MW00795073

There is nothing more importa
to God—and that is the big ic
terrific book by Gary Kendall. As you read the many stories of people embracing the Jesus mission you will find yourself inspired and wanting to give this book to inspire others.

—Dave Ferguson, Lead Pastor—Community Christian Church
Spiritual Entrepreneur—NewThing

Using the power of stories, Gary creatively helps people to understand what it is to "know" Jesus and in so doing how to become fulfilled in life. This is a book that is a great resource for an individual or group who longs to know their life's purpose. The stories alone are worth the purchase price.

—John Fozard, Ph.D, President Mid-America Christian University

Gary Kendall continues to prove why he is a gift to the church. His vision, leadership, and wisdom continue to help propel the Church forward. *Backwards* is one more significant way God is using Gary to help us go further faster. This book is a must read for those exploring faith, new to the faith, and anyone who may need challenged to a higher level of surrender to Christ. Get it. Read it. Live it.

—Tom Planck, Pastor, Church planter and coach HGCM

Gary expresses the questions many have and provides the answers we need. Drawing from his wealth of experiences in ministry, Gary has taken the fear and unknown out of giving yourself to the Lord with very practical methods. This book will both challenge you and encourage you to be one of Jesus' 21st century disciples reaching out to our post-Christian generation. It is guaranteed to make you a better disciple of our Lord.

—Donna Thomas, Founder Project Partner and
City Vision Ministries, Author

Gary Kendall has given his life to help people who are far from God, not just find their way back, but become fully devoted followers of Jesus Christ. He's more passionate about church planting and disciple-making than anyone I know. What he shares isn't theory, it's lessons learned from 30 years of raising up Christ followers.

—Steve Chiles, Pastor & Church Health Coach

I've often heard the phrase, "backwards about going forward" as it related to a person who was indecisive. However, this book brings new meaning to the word, "backwards" for me. My friend and author Gary Kendall has given motion and meaning to the joy of *Living Sent*. Written by a master discipler, this book is a must for every believer.

—Dr. Stan Toler
Bestselling Author
Oklahoma City, Oklahoma

It's rare to know someone who, throughout all the variations of life, seems to consistently and naturally live out of a core conviction. Gary Kendall is one of those people who consistently and in such natural ways lives his belief that people matter to God . . . and to him. "Backwards" is a perfect read for those who want to know that God and how they can live a life of difference.

—Tom Bassford, Founder of Significant Matters

I highly recommend this book for anyone with a genuine desire to know the heart of God the Father for your life and to experience His presence daily in your life. Pastor Gary Kendall has provided here a pathway to following God in full devotion that is very practical, down to earth, and engaging. Here in these pages there is hope for healing in our relationships and insightful keys to living a life that is exciting and full of adventure. Read this book and you will find your way back to God and you will be equipped to help others find their way back too!

—Gary Schmitz, Executive Director of Citywide Prayer K.C.

Gary writes about the spiritual journey in a down to earth, practical way that is both humorous and inspirational. His heart for connecting people to a real relationship with God is obvious. He's one who lives it.

—Russ Olmon, Founding President Ministry Advantage

backwards
Created to Live Sent

Discover the freedom and adventure of on-purpose living.

Gary Kendall

To find out more about Gary Kendall and the
Spiritual Growth Initiative, *30 Days to Living Sent,*
Please visit www.GaryKendall.org
and click on the SENT logo.

Copyright © 2012

ISBN: 978-1-937602-35-2

Dust Jacket Press
PO Box 721243
Oklahoma City, OK 73172
www.dustjacket.com <http://www.dustjacket.com>
800-495-0192

Cover Design: Tim Stout

To my friends at Indian Creek Community Church,
it is through you that God gave me the
primary context for what it means to live SENT.

contents

acknowledgements

I want to thank my wife Belinda for her tireless support as a wife. She is up for any wild adventure in serving Christ. I love what God is doing in us and I can't imagine a better life partner. She read and edited this project with great heart and skill.

My kids and their spouses share their time with me so I can live the life that is *SENT*. I truly appreciate their support and love. Kristen and Josh Levitt, Jeremy and Jesi Kendall, Luke and Rachel Kendall your grace toward me sets a wonderful context for life and ministry.

My Dad, Paul Kendall, was without a doubt the greatest impact on my love for people who don't yet know real life in Christ. His grace giving attitude is second to none. I can't thank him enough for all he instilled in me.

My Mom, Ruthie Kendall, is a spiritual cheerleader. She believes in me and she is not shy about telling anyone who will listen. She read and re-read the script, made suggestions and spoke many affirming words of inspiration.

Tim Stout supplied the artwork for the front and back cover in addition to the diagrams inside. Not only did he come up with great ideas and artistic design but he continually challenged my thinking to higher levels. He also keeps me grounded in reality.

This project took on a new urgency after a talk with Mark Batterson in the café at Indian Creek. He challenged me to start writing. He talked about the discipline of getting out what God put in. He gave me the push I needed to begin. I'll always thank him for it.

Jean Janner is a super Executive Assistant who keeps my schedule and tries to keep me on schedule. She understands my priorities and cleared space for this project.

The Leadership Team at Indian Creek encourages me to use the gifts God's given me and to lead beyond Indian Creek. John Bennie, Ben Stears and Steve Southards inspire me and keep me grounded at the same time. I love the teamwork and ministry we share.

My friends and co-workers at Healthy Growing Churches continually encouraged me to reach out to those who needed to hear this message. Patsy Wootton, Tom Planck, Greg Wiens and all—thanks for the wind in my sail.

Robin Wood keeps calling out the gift in me to write. Many times he pushed me to tell the story of what God is doing in me and through Indian Creek Community Church. I thank God for his friendship and his ministry.

Adam Toler and DustJacket have been great partners in this project. Stan Toler first told me about your ministry and he was right on target. Keep up the good work.

introduction

I write to those who don't yet know real life in Jesus. I want you to understand that even though from birth forward it feels right to look out for self that there is a better way. It might seem backwards initially to follow Jesus but you were created in the image of God for relationship with Him. Once you experience the richness of this life with him you will decide that doing life on your own is what is truly backwards. I believe you will find yourself saying, I was made for this!

Some may be reading who've just made this choice to follow Christ and I say with confidence, the best is yet to come! Once you find your way back to God then keep growing to become like Jesus. Yes, it is possible. This is why I write.

It helps me to break this journey into steps and I've used a circle to illustrate it. When you begin following you make a choice to enter relationship with Jesus. I call that finding your way back to God. As you continue in the relationship you grow to be like him. Three steps along the way are to learn to love God, love people and to live out the love of Jesus. Each leads to the other and in the process you discover you are meant to live life on purpose, on mission all the time. I call that living *SENT*. When these converge is when you live most like Jesus.

Jesus said this to his followers, *As the Father has sent me so I send you.* He invites us to live *SENT* just like he did. You'll love it when you live it. This is why I write. Join me in the journey of *Backwards: Created to Live SENT.*

Gary Kendall

find your way back to God and become like Christ

live SENT

chapter 1

backwards

"The trouble with a mule is that he's
backward about going forward."

—Vance Havner

Does it ever feel like something's backwards? Life's not working for you, and you don't know why.

Imagine this. The beautiful blue Caribbean ocean. No clouds in sight. Gentle tropical breezes. The surf's up. It's another day in paradise.

However, my life wasn't picture perfect. The idea seemed innocent enough, but the result was more telling than I could know. My wife, Belinda, and I were on vacation. We set out that day with eight other couples to kayak along the coast of an island and to enjoy a leisurely day surrounded by absolute beauty. What could be better than that?

We listened to the details of how to get the kayak off the beach and avoid capsizing when the first set of waves crested near the shore, but we couldn't agree on what we had just heard. The surf was loud and adrenaline was pumping. Belinda was nervous because she doesn't swim well. I was overconfident because I grew up in Alaska, had spent a lot of time in a canoe, and knew we would be just fine.

As we pushed off from the shore, I said, *you paddle on the right* (her strong side), *and I will paddle on the left*. The first big wave came at us and she paddled frantically on the right and then switched to the left. I tried to correct her verbally and offset her choices by paddling opposite her. That didn't work because she kept changing sides. I didn't know which way she was going next. I tried desperately to guess and keep us headed straight into the first big wave. To turn sideways into the wave would be certain disaster.

The bow went straight up in the air. The surf splashed in our faces. We went down the other side with incredible speed. Somehow we made it past the first wave upright. We were off on a great adventure! Life is good! We can do this, or so we thought.

Then the struggle for control set in. We argued about how to steer the kayak and who should take which role. I complained that everyone else seemed to have it figured out. And notice they were cooperating. They were even smiling and enjoying the experience. That didn't help us.

The guide instructed us as a group to follow him in a line parallel to the shoreline. We were not only falling to the back of the line, which was a problem for me, but he was so far ahead we could barely see him. After some animated discussion, Belinda told me if I was so smart I could just paddle by myself and see how that worked. I said, *that would be an improvement*. Belinda decided she had had enough and quit paddling completely. Out of frustration I quit paddling too.

dead in the water

Dead in the water. That's what happens if you don't paddle. Then the sea takes you wherever it wants you to go. That was not good!

We made apologies and started again. We tried harder. We tried a LOT harder. By now the sun was blazing hot. The sky was a beautiful blue, but there were no clouds. The fun factor was fading fast. We were far from shore. Belinda kept reminding me the water was deep and there were sharks. We couldn't go back to where we had started. If we didn't find a way to paddle together soon we would lose sight of everyone else. Besides, finishing last wasn't an option in my book! What do you do when what you thought would be great fun takes a disastrous turn?

our only choice

Considering our alternatives were limited, we did what we had to do. We quit complaining. We stopped fighting each other. Belinda started paddling again, and I paddled opposite her changing when she changed. We improved enough to steer in the general direction. Over time we began to catch up with the others. We wouldn't win a prize for our tactics, but with two strong wills, we found a way to make it work. I started counting how many kayaks were ahead of us. Maybe if we made it a race it would be more fun. Belinda didn't care about a race and wasn't buying.

Since there was plenty of time, we did eventually catch and pass every kayak except one. I must admit that I was pretty proud when we caught that last wave and coasted onto the beach. The guide grabbed the front of our kayak to steady it so we could get out. Then the guide peered at us with an astonished look on his face and exclaimed, *in all my years I've never seen that before! You traveled the whole trip going backwards! How did you do that?*

Good question! No wonder it was so hard! Just so you know, both ends of the boat came to a point. Evidently, we were supposed to get in the kayak facing the shore. We didn't know that. When you push off backwards the first thing you do is turn toward the waves. We got into the kayak facing the waves and took off. I guess we should have listened to our guide more closely! Suddenly, the struggle for the last hour and one half made a lot more sense.

harder than it should be

Maybe you know the feeling that life seems harder than it should be. Maybe you missed the details or someone else in your world isn't cooperating. It isn't unusual that what appears to be a rather simple and fun exercise of living instead turns into an unexpected ordeal.

What if you got it fundamentally backwards? What if you think you are supposed to be leading in life and in reality you were designed to follow?

it is all about me

It's normal to live your life believing you were born to be in control. Isn't life all about you? It is about having what you want and the freedom to do as you please—that's what brings happiness. Isn't that what we think from the cradle forward? The problem is that it doesn't work so well in everyday life. Before long you find yourself arguing, competing, and complaining with others who believe the same thing—that it is all about them. And after you've both tried harder AND threatened to quit, you eventually come to the place where you are dead in the water.

I'm not the fastest or brightest student of life, or kayaking, but I've come to an astonishing discovery: I am made for more than that! And you are too. There is a better way!

Life is better when you turn around and go the direction the Guide advises. You slice through the water. Steering is easier. Your efforts are more productive. You get along with others better. You can enjoy the journey.

In this book we discover the benefit of living life, not backwards but as God designed. It is a life that is filled with on purpose living. This brings great adventure and amazing satisfaction.

backwards, chapter 1
questions for thought and discussion

1. Give an example of a time when it seemed like things were backwards for you.

2. How are you dealing with things that aren't working for you?

3. What might be backwards for you?

4. What do you think the guide would say to you about how to find a better way to travel through life?

finding my way

Knowing where you are going is found in the words
of Jesus, "I am the way, the truth and the life."
—John Fozard

This backwards story is a lot like my life and maybe yours too.
I've wasted a lot of effort going the wrong way, my way, before
turning around and discovering God had a better plan.

This book describes how to find your way back to God and
become like Jesus. I call this living a life that is *SENT*. This may
be a new way to use the word *sent* and a new concept for living.
It may sound backwards but consider the alternative—living a life
that's all about self. How is that working for you? It didn't work so
well for me. As much as you try, you just can't get the rest of the
world to cooperate and support your plan when it is all about
you.

a higher purpose

What if there is a higher purpose for you and your life? Are you going about it backwards? What if you turn around and go God's way? Instead of calling the shots you learn to cooperate with the Designer of life. You learn to follow His lead. Give this thought some time to sink in.

Life begins to make sense when you discover the very reason for which you were created. It isn't always easy, but it begins to work. Relationships become sweeter. You start to enjoy the journey and in the process you come to the conclusion—I believe I was made for this!

turn around

Life is meant to be guided by the One who loves you so much He not only created you but died to recover relationship with you. This love is amazing! You give up your need to do things your way. You acknowledge you are living for self and you turn around. God in His Word, the Bible, uses the word *repent* for this turn around. In the Greek language, the word for *repent* is *metanoeo*, and it means to turn around and go the complete opposite direction. It is like doing a 180 degree U-turn.

It is like you were sitting backwards in the boat. You choose to accept the leadership of Jesus based not on what you can do but on what He's already done for you on the cross. You invite Him to lead, and you chose to follow. The surroundings haven't changed yet, but you are reoriented. It is a whole new way of living.

Following initially feels like relearning how to sit in the boat and paddle. But rather quickly it feels like a fit. Before long you become a raving fan. And soon you are on a mission to tell the world there is a better way. You find yourself living *SENT*—there is purpose, there is a plan, and you want everyone to find what you've found.

When Jesus invited His disciples into a new way of living He said, *"Follow me and I will send you out to fish for people."*[1] We follow not to serve ourselves but to be *sent* out for others. Our lives take on the focus of Jesus' life. It sounds backwards, doesn't it?

Many people think religion is adding another piece to the pie of life. You've got your friends, family, a job, a place to live, an education, a doctor, and now we add to this list of resources the help of God. It's like finding the bottle with the genie!

While this thinking may be a starting place, it is much less than what God has in mind for you. He wants you to follow Him in a life that is wholly devoted to the adventure He has for you. It is important to realize the end from the beginning. What He wants is for you to follow Him and become like Him.

The heart of God's hope for you is healed relationships with God and others. It is a life that is other oriented.

This life is exciting too! You are invited to surrender your will and join God in the grand purpose of life which is to rescue a world of people doing life backwards. That is what Jesus meant when He said you would be sent to fish for men. When you find your way back to God, you are sent to others with a message of reconciliation. You will be helping others find their way back to God to become like Jesus.

Before you there is the opportunity of a lifetime—to be in relationship with Jesus and to grow to be like Him! You become filled with His love for helping others find what you've found! It feels like you've turned the kayak around. This is how it was meant to be in the first place.

you can do it!

You can do it! You were made for this. This is *Good News!* It is powerful and divine. It changes you supernaturally from the inside out. You become a new person. You can't do it on your own, but the good news is God does it in you and through you.

Read about the dramatic turn-around story in the life of the Apostle Paul. He thought God was all about rules and control until God confronted him with the truth. Paul went from persecuting followers of Jesus to living a life sent to proclaim freedom and grace. This is what he wrote about the transformation in his life: *This means that anyone who belongs to Christ has become a new person. The old life is gone; a new life has begun!* [2]

is it Time for a change?

Is it time for a change? Do you need a turn-around story for your life? Do you feel drawn to God's love? Invite God to reveal Himself to you right now. Your heart might beat a little faster realizing that God is real, but that's a good thing. He is inviting you to follow Him right now. Do it! Say, *Yes* to His invitation.

He does for you what you can't do for yourself. He redeems all that is good in you, and He cleans out what doesn't belong. Will you let Him do that for you?

my Story

I remember very clearly the day I made this choice. I felt drawn to accept Jesus' love at the end of a church service. It both scared me and excited me. The speaker presented a life that was led by God. It was new to me, and I didn't know what to do with it. I felt claustrophobic. I wanted to get out of the auditorium, but I didn't want to draw attention to myself. I endured the last words of the song, and when the service was over, I looked for a place to get away. It was cold outside, so I went downstairs. Then I saw it—a restroom. It was a one-holer with a lock on the door, but that would have to do. I went inside and stood there not knowing what to do next.

Feeling foolish and embarrassed, I wondered what was happening inside me. In a moment of clarity, it occurred to me that I was running from a feeling; maybe even running from God. If it was God Who was pursuing me, I had to ask myself why I was running. It would be futile to try to get away from Him. At the same time, I was feeling inner conviction I would carry it with me wherever I went. I didn't know what I was afraid of. I did know that I needed help. I wasn't satisfied with life as I knew it, so why not invite Jesus to forgive me and lead me.

i used the toilet like an altar

I knelt on the floor using the toilet like an altar. I know it sounds silly, and I admit it felt a little bit awkward. Suddenly, I realized this was important, supremely urgent, and I wanted to symbolize the sincerity in my heart by kneeling.

I didn't know how to pray, so I just said what was on my heart. I asked Jesus to forgive me for my sin. I asked Him to come into my heart and lead my life. When I said *Amen* I had a great sense of peace come over me. I felt clean on the inside and out. I knew in that moment I found what my heart desired.

it is for you

You can find what I found. Open your heart to God and tell Him what you want and need. Invite Him to forgive you and to lead you. Accept His grace and forgiveness. You'll never regret it, and one day you'll look back on that moment and know it was the best choice you ever made. Stop traveling through life backwards.

a prayer for forgiveness

Jesus take the lead. Forgive me for going my own way (the Bible calls that sin). Turn me around and reorient me to live life like You designed it to be lived. I realize the life I'm living isn't enough. Fill me with Your strength and love. I choose to follow. Live in me and through me so I can become all You want me to be. Give me Your love for others. I accept your mission. Help me live a life that is SENT. Amen.

Jesus said this to His disciples, *Peace be with you! As the Father has sent me, I am sending you.*[3]

Now, let's discover the adventure of living a life that is *SENT!*

finding my way, chapter 2
questions for thought and discussion

1. What does the word *metanoeo* imply?

2. Do you think it is possible to come to God and not *repent*?

3. Jesus says, *Follow Me and I will make you fishers of people.*[4] What are the two parts of this invitation? Which part is your part and which part is God's?

4. Have you considered accepting the invitation of Jesus to forgive your sin and lead your life?

5. In light of this chapter, what is a next step for you?

footnotes
1. Mark 1:18 NIV
2. 2 Corinthians 5:17 NLT
3. John 20:20 NIV
4. Mark 1:18 NIV

i can't do it

"Don't be afraid to ask for help.
We were not created to do life alone."

—Belinda Kendall

Everyone eventually comes to the place where they meet their own mortality and realize they can't do life alone. That time came for me at 2 a.m. in the morning, May 21. I couldn't sleep because the pain was too great. My mind was racing and it wouldn't stop no matter how much I prayed. Belinda was crashed on the couch in the living room. We both were dealing with grievous tragedy. Our precious baby daughter, Megan, 21, months old, had died in her sleep the previous morning. We had been left to do the unthinkable, to put the pieces of our lives back together without our youngest child.

In my grief I cried out to God. It was incredulous to me that He had allowed Megan to die. How could He? It wasn't that I thought I was so righteous but she was so young and innocent!

My heart hurt beyond whatever capacity for pain I thought I had. I don't know that I really expected to hear anything back from Him; venting was more of what I had in mind.

But in the darkness of that moment, in my spirit, I heard something I believe came from God, *I know how you feel, my Son died too.*

That got my attention! I sat up. Was God speaking to me in a spiritual way? Once I recovered from the surprise, it brought me comfort to know God was there with me in the pain. I felt His peace. He said He understood. I didn't hear condemnation for my doubt. I felt His compassion in a way that words don't describe.

After a brief pause the thought continued, *And I willingly sent My Son to die so you could live.*

I knew mentally that Jesus died on the cross for the sin of the world. But now that I knew what it felt like to lose someone I loved—it was unthinkable that God would willingly choose for His only Son to die. Yet that is exactly the choice the Father God made. He sent His Son Jesus to pay for the sin of the world. Incredible! The love of God was never more real to me than it was at that moment. I felt His presence and His comfort was salve to my soul.

I wasn't looking for an explanation. I needed to know that there is a God who loves and that He would come near. He wasn't distant. He was close. He wasn't unfeeling. His heart shared hurt with mine. He didn't condemn me. He joined me.

I couldn't do it alone but with His help I could face the new day. I accurately understood that our family would never be the same. So with His daily presence we walked slowly and with faltering steps into a new normal. We learned there is a God who cares and comes near.

don't do life alone

You aren't created to do life alone either. I was tempted to doubt whether God had my best interests in mind. I wasn't sure I could trust Him. But He knew exactly where I was and what I was going through. He knew how to reach me and He did.

I've heard it said, *when you can't find God start praying and He will find you.* That was true in my case.

God carried me and my family through the grieving process and over time brought us to a place of healing. We've shared generously with others what we learned in our grief. Day by day God brought truth and people into our lives who led us lovingly into restoration. We will always miss Megan but we are no longer debilitated and we are stronger for our loss. It is a great consolation to know we will be reunited with her in heaven. We are looking forward to living together in eternity with her and with Jesus.

I regularly doubt things, often as an exercise in searching for truth, but I've not doubted since that day that God's posture toward me is love. This is true for you too. He loves you. I realized then that what God wants from us is for us to trust Him and to love Him in return.

it's all about relationship

Here is the great truth I've learned about life—it is all about relationship. God wants relationship with me and with you. To get the most out of life we will want to learn to relate well with others. If we don't do relationships well we won't do life well.

When Jesus came to teach us how to find relationship with the Father and Holy Spirit He did it by calling disciples to share life with Him. The best learning always comes with application in relationship. He didn't simply point them to His Word, the scriptures, He lived truth out in their presence. John, one of his disciples, called him a living word.

you are designed for relationship

I know this about you even if I don't know you well or even at all—you were not created to live life alone. You too will come to times when you can't do it. God designed you to desire relationship with Him. Without Him there is a God shaped hole in your soul.

He is the One who thought up relationships with others, some of whom will become family, friends and community. Sharing community is what makes life sweeter. In relationships the joys are multiplied and the sorrows are shared.

You need God and you need others. Life will prove that to you over the course of time. But why wait for that day?

living *SENT*

When you follow Jesus, you find life as it was meant to be. There is a harmony in loving God, loving people and living out the love of Jesus. I call that living the life that is *SENT*

I'm a visual guy. It helps me understand things when I draw pictures of how they relate. Here is how I picture the life Jesus wants us to live.

love God

Inside of one circle it says *Love God*. A big part of your life is learning to accept the love of God and in doing so you learn to relate to Him. Jesus gave us two Great Commandments. The first is to *Love the Lord your God with all your heart and with all your soul and with all your mind.*[1]

love people

The second circle speaks to human relationships. Jesus spoke of the importance of building strong relationships when he gave what is called the Great Commandment, to *love your neighbor as yourself.*[2] Loving people is a joy and a challenge. It is often what we love most about life and at the same time what challenges us to our core.

live out

The third circle depicts an aspect of life that we don't always acknowledge. Jesus spoke of it when He said, *It is more blessed to give than to receive.*[3] We are called to live out the love of Jesus and when we do we are satisfied at a soul level.

SENT

The three circles intersect. This place in the middle connects all three and is at the same time a part of each. It represents an integration of life that looks like the lifestyle of Jesus. If we could live in this place it would be to live like Jesus. Since He lived this holistic life and He was sent from the Father to do so I call this place living the life that is *SENT.*

Here one lives in a right relationship with God and with others. We are not living for self but for His higher purpose. The result of this motivation is that you live out the love of Jesus. This is why you were created. You were made not to serve self but to live SENT.

Heaven touches earth in this place where divine power intersects our lives. There is healing in relationships and there is freedom from selfishness when we live life on mission. The return cycle in serving is a natural high.

This is the mission of Jesus—to help you discover life as it was meant to be. He put it this way in His keynote address delivered in his home town of Nazareth. *The Spirit of the Sovereign Lord is on me, because the Lord has anointed me to proclaim good news to the poor. He has sent me to bind up the brokenhearted, to proclaim freedom for the captives and release from darkness for the prisoners, to proclaim the year of the Lord's favor.*[4]

It's Jesus' desire that each of us receives the good news and discovers the healing He offers. Just like Jesus was sent to deliver this good news and invite others to find and follow Him—so are you! He came to make disciples who would then make disciples until the whole world knows.

If you are not living the SENT life you aren't living life to the fullest! The culture tells us, *Look out for yourself. Live for the moment. Put yourself first. Be your own boss.* But Jesus tells us there is a better way than to simply gratify ourselves. He said, *I have come that they might have life, and have it to the full.*[5] He told us how when He said, *As the Father has sent me, so I am sending you.*[6]

jon and glynis dewitt

My good friends, Jon and Glynis DeWitt, are great examples of two people who turned from living for self to living lives that are SENT.

When I first came to know my friends I often saw Jon and Glynis at my neighbor's pool. Jon was the life of the party. He'd play pool volleyball with a beer in his hand and a quick quip that kept everyone laughing. Every time I talked with Jon he was kind but it was clear that he didn't think he needed God.

What looked like fun and success on the outside was actually eating him up on the inside. He later admitted that much of the chasing after good times, women (before Glynis) and money was a cover up for the emptiness he felt inside. Jon and Glynis hit bottom when their relationship deteriorated to the point that the future for them looked bleak. Life is all about relationships, isn't it? When they aren't working we are miserable. Jon and Glynis were miserable.

Jon found his way back to God. One night he spent several hours on his face in his basement crying out to God for forgiveness and for help to reconcile with Glynis. God met him there with open arms and relationship with God was reborn. Jon was a new man inside and out. He's still the life of any party, but the party that is his life now has a new purpose.

I'll never forget the Monday morning when I heard a knock at my front door at about 8:00 o'clock. It was Jon.

What am I supposed to do? He asked?

I too was confused because I didn't know the back story yet. I invited him in and he began to describe the changes that had occurred in his heart. He wanted everyone to know the new life he found in Jesus. He was ready to go door to door telling everyone. We prayed together to seal his commitment and then we asked God for direction. I wish you could have seen us. We were two grown men hugging and wiping tears of joy! I encouraged Jon to start by telling his own family before he went door to door.

Glynis, Jon's wife, was skeptical. She wanted to see if the change was real. Would it last? She kept her distance for weeks but the change was so deep and profound that she wanted to find her way back to God too. She found my wife Belinda one Sunday and poured out her heart to God. She experienced forgiveness so profound it overwhelmed her. She accepted amazing grace and received a peace all at once in a time she will never forget. Glynis now finds joy serving alongside Jon leading an Alpha group. But perhaps her greatest joy is mentoring other young women to turn around and find what she found in relationship with Jesus.

Jon knew he was sent to tell others but it wasn't by knocking on doors in our neighborhood. He started putting together a daily devotional he sends out to anyone interested. The last count I heard he had over 1,400 people receiving the *devos* as he calls them. Many of them pass them on to a network of friends and the chain reaches around the world.

admit it

You can discover the relationship Jon and Glynis found if you'll admit you can't do it alone. I say it this way, *I can't but He can!* He won't wrestle control away from you. If you will reach for Him you'll discover He was already there reaching for you.

let's pray

Jesus, please take over. I admit I can't do life without You. I recognize that You take on the responsibility to recreate Your life in me. Thank You. I give you my full cooperation. I want to live SENT. Fill me up with more of You. Thank You that You have my best interest in mind. Reorient me to love God, love people and live out Your love. I'm excited to begin living the SENT life! Amen

i can't do it! chapter 3
questions for thought or discussion

1. Can you think of a time when God met you in your grief? How?

2. Does the phrase, *If you can't find God start praying and He will find you* encourage you? Why?

3. *Life is all about relationship,* do you agree or disagree?

4. How are your relationships with God and with others?

5. Review the three circles. The circles represent various parts of your life. Which of the areas in your life is the strongest? Which is weakest?

6. The area in the center of the circle represents living a life that is like Jesus. We call that living *SENT*. How are you doing in learning to live sent?

7. What will you do now with what you've learned?

footnotes

1. Matthew 22:37 NIV
2. Matthew 22:39 NIV
3. Acts 20:35 NLT
4. Isaiah 61:1-2 NIV
5. John 10:10 NIV
6. John 20:21 NLT

chapter 4

embrace the journey

"Tough circumstances and grief take all of us on
different journeys with similar characteristics."
—Mary Beth Chapman

I grew up in Alaska, the son of a missionary couple, Paul and
Ruthie Kendall. We spent two of our summers before I was sixteen
crisscrossing the *lower 48* to raise funds. I was still a young man
when I could say I'd been to 49 states (Hawaii had to wait). That
adds up to a lot of time in the car together!

My dad was old school when it came to traveling. In his mind
you drew a line from where you were to where you wanted to go.
Everything was focused on the destination. We learned to hold
it—you know what I mean. And when we did stop, we attempted
to set a new record for the fastest pit stop. We got gas, food, and
did our business in record time. Occasionally, we even timed our
stops. You got to relax when we arrived at our destination; until
then it was full speed ahead.

One summer we were traveling on the Alcan Highway just out-side Dawson Creek, Canada, when I received a strange prompting. It was a thought that seemed to come out of nowhere. We had just stopped to eat lunch at an A &W Root Beer Drive In. Afterwards, we piled back into the car, and when we did, I traded seats so that I was sitting in the front seat on the passenger side.

A few miles down the road we saw a sign that said, *Buckle your seat belt. Someone loves you.*Being a young teen I was squarely in the middle of adolescence. I immediately countered with the thought, *No one loves me.*That wasn't true, but I didn't have a girl friend I reasoned to myself. That thought among oth-ers led me to question whether I was loved. Then the thought came again, *buckle your seatbelt God loves you.* That motivated me to action, so I buckled my seatbelt.

Before long we passed a pickup truck with four teens jammed into the cab: two guys and two girls. They were poking along like they had something other than driving on their minds. The next thing we knew, they had stepped on the gas and passed us. When they did, they all turned around and looked and stared at us. We thought maybe they saw our Alaska license plate and they wanted to see if we looked like Eskimos. Or perhaps the teenage driver was just filled with testosterone and wanted to show off by passing the family station wagon. Once they passed us they slowed down again.

Assuming that they made their point, my dad pulled up beside them to pass them back. We were about a foot ahead of them when they made a left-hand turn directly into the front quarter panel of our car. They struck our vehicle literally a foot from where I sat. The contact drove us off the road into a ditch. We hit the ground without the benefit of time for my dad to hit the brake. We were probably traveling nearly 70 miles an hour at impact. The sudden impact propelled my brother forward from the very back of the car where he had laid down to sleep on top of the suitcases. Miraculously, my Dad caught him before he hit the windshield. It was a reflex action, but it saved my brother Brad's life.

The car was a wreck, but we survived—all of us. My dad had bruises from the steering wheel. My mom was bruised from hitting the back seat. Brad was sore from his flight through the air which came to an abrupt stop. I survived without bruises or injuries. You couldn't even tell that I was in a wreck. As I climbed out my door, I remembered the sign we passed a few miles earlier. I recalled that I had put on my seatbelt because I was reminded that God loved me. At that same moment, a thought dropped in my mind, the thought was, *I have a plan for your life.* I think the thought came from God.

My family had an unexpected stay in Dawson Creek, Canada. But eventually we got our car fixed, and we continued our trip. You could probably guess how an accident like this affected us. We decided that life wasn't just about getting from point A to B. We would still have to travel, but this was a huge reminder that there was more to life than just passing through. We decided we wanted to enjoy the journey. Life is too short and relationships are too precious just to get from here to there.

For the purpose of full disclosure, my dad still found a way to average just short of 700 miles a day, but we learned to enjoy the journey. We played games in the car. We prayed. We sang. We read stories. We had fun being together. We listened to ball games and books on tape. I know I'm dating myself but you get the point. We changed our focus, and we've never been sorry. It seemed like the time went faster. And guess what? We still made it on time!

are you racing through life?

You may not be physically racing through your life, but how many times do you approach life as if the clock is ticking to accumulate as many possessions and experiences as possible? When I began living *SENT* I learned to embrace the journey. You have a great eternal destination, but learn to enjoy the life God's given you here!

life is a journey

Life is a journey. Growth often involves a process where one insight needs time and space for the next one to make sense. And spiritual formation is like that. Many truths need to sit on top of another to be fully grasped. Often there is a stepwise manner in which the lessons unfold. Usually it isn't linear, and it is uniquely different for each of us, but growth in maturity follows a predictable learning process.

You may find the following spiritual formation diagram helpful. It describes four different places on the spiritual journey.

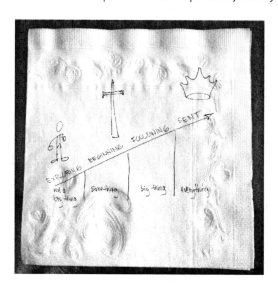

exploring

We all start here. We don't know what we think about God. Maybe we've never heard God's story before. Or perhaps this is the first time we've considered the fact that we are spiritual beings. At this place we might think, *I am not sure what I think about God and Christianity.* We are exploring the idea but haven't made a choice to choose God's way. This person might describe their spiritual journey like this, *Faith is not a significant part of my life.* God is nothing specific to this person.

beginning

The next place in our journey and in our diagram is the place where a person says, *I believe in Jesus, and I am learning what it means to get to know Him.* This person has made a choice to identify with Jesus and accept His invitation to forgiveness and grace. God is a part of their life. He is something, but it is early enough that it is not yet clear exactly what this choice means. This person is excited about the journey, but they are just beginning.

following

The third place in the journey is where we welcome Jesus into our daily life and ask Him to influence the direction of it. We ask Him to lead us and we are willing to follow. This person says, *I depend on Christ for daily guidance. I get closer to Him through regular spiritual practices. I'm learning what it means to be in relationship.* At this time in a person's life, God is not just something, God is a big thing. Because of Him they are gaining ground in learning to love God, love people, and live out the love of Jesus.

SENT

The next place in our spiritual journey is where we make a very significant decision. We could say it like this, *I will not only follow Christ, but I will dedicate myself to allow Him to replicate His life in mine.* At this point, we are beginning to live *SENT.* God is everything to the person living *SENT.*

which best describes you?

Where do you find yourself today? Where are you in your spiritual journey? What points have you experienced along the way? Just like children go through a maturation process as they grow, our spiritual life grows. The rate of spiritual growth is personal and unique. But most of us go through a spiritual formation that resembles the diagram depicted here.

it requires cooperation

It is important to note that, unlike children, who grow naturally over time followers of Christ don't grow unless they cooperate with the Holy Spirit. Growth comes only through staying connected in relationship.

You will go through the various points at your own speed, and in some cases, it may even seem that you skip one. No illustration perfectly replicates spiritual formation. However, you can use the diagram as a point of reference to where you are today. And you can compare it to where you want to go.

Let's make some personal applications. Ask God *if He is real to reveal Himself to you in some way that you can't manufacture.*It is amazing how God shows up when you least expect Him! Expect Him to validate His presence to you, and He will!

steve papa

My friend, Steve Papa, told me he didn't want to ever talk about spiritual things again. And this was after we'd been friends for seven years. That hurt! In order to preserve the relationship, I agreed to never talk to him about spiritual things if he would do one thing for me. *What is that? He asked.*

I said, *You don't believe in God because you've never given Him a chance. You say you don't believe in the Bible, but you've never read it. Let me give you some scriptures to read. Read them and pray to the God you don't believe in (but play along) and ask with sincerity that if He is real He will reveal Himself to you.*

To which he replied, *You're on!*

We met a few days later to start the challenge. I assigned Steve several scriptures to read including, *God so loved the world that he gave his one and only son, that whoever believes in him shall not perish but have eternal life.*[1] I wanted him to know the best news the world has ever heard. I gave it to him not knowing that God had a surprise for both of us.

how did you know?

When Steve and I met again, he greeted me with this question, *How did you know?*

This launched a comical conversation where I tried to convince him I didn't know something he thought I knew. Finally, I got it out of him. He wanted to know how I knew that he was really ticked off at his brother. They had traded harsh words and nearly fought.

I didn't know that, I attempted to reassure him. *But why do you think I did?*

Because of what you told me to read, came the answer. In my mind I did a quick review of the text of scripture I gave him to read. I was unable to piece together why he would be so upset.

Show me what you read, I said. He pulled out an old, tiny, hand sized King James Bible and turned to a totally different text. However, the address of the text looked very similar. It was 1 John 3:16.

Steve had read from a book titled 1 John when I intended for him to read the one simply titled John. Suddenly I felt stupid. Why had I not prepared him better to find scriptures in the Bible? I should have covered that when I gave the assignment. How did I forget that? For a moment I beat myself up. He read the wrong scripture! Or did he?

real love

Here's what he read, *This is how we know what love is: Jesus Christ laid down his life for us. And we ought to lay down our lives for our brothers and sisters.*[2]

Did Linda (his wife) put you up to this, he asked me. It was obviously troubling him. I later learned he felt guilty for the way he was treating his brother.

Linda didn't put me up to this, I promised. He believed me.

Then Steve said, *I can't believe it! This book is full of scriptures and you chose the exact one that I needed to read.* He was giving me credit I didn't deserve.

Steve, I interrupted, *Don't give me credit for that. I gave you a different scripture. You are the one who read the wrong one. But I think I know Who chose that scripture for you.* I let the truth hang in the air for some time. Then continued, *God knew exactly*

44 | backwards

what you needed to hear and He led you to that verse to prove He exists.

I smiled to myself loving the way God works. *He's revealing Himself to you right now through these events,* I continued. *Don't you see, I gave you one verse but you looked up a different one? I didn't have a clue about your brother, but obviously you are feeling guilty. God knew how and where to speak to you. He wants you to let Him lead you.*

A few weeks later Steve's wife, Linda, had the privilege of helping Steve find his way back to God. For the next seven years or so, Steve and Linda worked with the student ministry in their church helping others find what they had found.

how steve found his way back to God

In conversation with Linda, Steve discovered Jesus had done everything that needed to be done for us to be in right relationship with God. That is His gift to us. But to receive it you must do what only you can do, which is to accept God's forgiveness and grace. You do this by acknowledging you went your own way through self-ishness and sin. Repent of going your own self-directed way and invite Him to lead your life.

If you haven't yet made this choice already, take a moment now and pray. You can use three word or phrases we learn as children to begin the prayer, *sorry, thank you and please.*

sorry

Lord Jesus, I'm sorry that I went my own way. I realize you call that sin, and I repent of that now and turn toward You.

thank you

Thank You for dying on the cross for my sin and the sin of the whole world. I accept that You died for me. I receive Your forgiveness and grace.

please live in me

Please live in me and form the nature of Christ in me. I invite You to lead me. Take out the backwards, selfish thinking and turn me around so I can live in a way that is pleasing to You. I want to live the life of one who is SENT. Amen.

a child of God

When you make this choice several things happen. Your sins are forgiven, and you are washed clean on the inside. God adds you to His family. You become a child of God. The Bible says it like this, *To all who believed him and accepted him, he gave the right to become children of God.*[3]

You are instantly in right standing with God. A divine trade takes place. Jesus takes on your sin and you receive His purity. This is an incredible deal! You trade places. From now on when the Father looks at you He sees the righteousness of Christ in you.

the Holy Spirit

You are given the Spirit of Jesus, the Holy Spirit, to live inside your spirit. He is your constant guide and companion. This concept confused me. Growing up, I often heard the Holy Spirit referred to as the Holy Ghost. I didn't want any part of any ghost. It was also troubling to me that another spirit could live inside me.

As I searched the Bible on my own as an adult, it occurred to me that the Holy Spirit was simply Jesus without a human body.

All of us are both body and spirit. Your spirit is what makes you—you. It is a combination of your soul, your intellect, your character, and your life experiences. The Bible teaches that when your human body dies your spirit lives on in eternity. That's good news as long as you are in right relationship with God.

When Jesus died, was resurrected, and later ascended to heaven He sent His Spirit to be with His disciples. His Spirit lives inside every Christ follower.

a lesson from a balloon

This illustration helped me understand how the Holy Spirit works inside us. You can blow up a balloon with your breath. When you are done, if you let go, it floats to the floor. But the balloon is created with the capacity to hold more. You could put helium in the balloon and when you let go it will rise instead of fall. From the beginning of time you were made in the image of God with the capacity for the Spirit of God to live in you. Your spirit and His Spirit can both share your spiritual being. This was God's original design and plan.

Through our sinful choices we left God out and as a result the balloon that is our spirit couldn't stay up on its own. Left to ourselves we sink. But when we accept the invitation of Jesus, the Holy Spirit of God takes His rightful place in us and we soar. When He lives in us we can live the *SENT* life because we have the Spirit of Jesus living in us. The Bible says, *when you believed, you were marked in him with a seal, the promised Holy Spirit.*[4]

One of the most amazing things to me about the presence of the Holy Spirit's power in our lives is that it is instantaneous and gradual. We have all of Him from the beginning. You get every-thing He is. The question is: Does He have all of you?

grace undeserved

You won't get it right every day and for that there is grace. Remind yourself frequently, I wasn't forgiven by my own merit. It wasn't about what I did. It was about what He did for me and for you. And the same grace that saved you is available now to foster a growing relationship. *God saved you by his grace when you believed. And you can't take credit for this; it is a gift from God.*[5]

Since this is a relationship, we don't want to take advantage of the grace of God. We want to live in a way that is pleasing to Him and honors Him. Even though grace is free to us it came at a high cost to Jesus. So when you do revert to selfishness and sin admit it. Ask for His help. Embrace grace and keep moving for-ward. This is why Jesus died, so you could live.

you can do it

You can do it because Jesus lives in you, and He will get you to the finish line. God is good at what He does, which is to redeem your life. You are a trophy of His grace. Relax into His care and trust the process He has for you. Embrace the journey. *I am certain that God, who began the good work within you, will continue his work until it is finally finished on the day when Christ Jesus returns.*[6]

SENT

And this is not all. A whole journey awaits you. The rest of the book describes what it is like to live a life that is SENT. Keep reading!

a prayer for grace

Jesus, thank You for loving me and living in me. I want to grow to be more like You. I want to live the SENT life where You are everything to me. Thank You for relating to me through grace. I want to walk in Your victory and live it out in such a way that others are inspired to follow You. Amen

embrace the journey, chapter 4
questions for thought or discussion

1. What were family trips like for you when you were growing up? Or if it is more relevant what are they like for you now?

2. How have you learned to embrace the journey?

3. Which of the four places in spiritual formation best represents where you are now, and why did you choose this one?

4. Have you chosen to accept the invitation of Jesus to live in His grace? When and what led up to that?

5. Are you learning to embrace the grace of God? How?

footnotes
1. John 3:16 NIV
2. 1 John 3:16 NIV
3. John 1:12 NLT
4. Ephesians 1:13 NIV
5. Ephesians 2:8, 9NLT
6. Philippians 1:6 NLT

love God

surprised by love

"Every normal man or woman longs more keenly for love,
for warm friendships and human responsiveness
more than anything else in life."

-Leslie B. Salter

The lunchroom was packed. The new school year at Gulf-Coast Bible College had started days earlier. Some students were in the lunch room to see if the food was edible. Others went to meet the new crop of students. After I went through the line to fill my plate, I stood for some time looking for a place to sit. Finally, I saw the only two open spaces in the room; they were immediately across from each other. I navigated my way through the chatty students and made my way to the seats. I sat my plate down to hold my spot and headed for the salad bar.

When I returned I noticed someone had the same idea and had captured the other open space. I didn't give it much thought. I had a lot on my mind and my main goal that day was to eat then get on to the more exciting parts of the day. I was barely seated when a cute girl with green eyes and long blonde hair sat down across from me. I learned her name was Belinda, and she was from Kentucky.

The day had just gotten better! I remembered seeing her at the Freshman Orientation a few days earlier. In that setting, I had teased her by telling her I was a brother to my good friend, Steve Chiles. She had bought it, and Steve and I had some fun with it later that evening. The two of us were there because we were Residence Assistants and served as hosts for the event. I assumed Belinda was there because she was a freshman.

I filed away some basic information. She had a charming hillbilly twang that was easy to like. She drove a hot car. It was one of my favorites, a black '76 Monte Carlo. Who wouldn't notice that? But after all she was a freshman, I thought. I wasn't looking for a relationship. I decided I'd enjoy the conversation over lunch and then get on with the rest of my day.

The first thing that I learned was that she was a transfer student from Morehead, KY. She wasn't a freshman she was a senior. That sounded a little more promising. She was working on a double major in Psychology and English Literature.

This might have some potential. The more I learned the more I liked. We sat and talked for a long time. Eventually, the lunch room emptied around us, and we hardly noticed.

Neither of us had the other at *Hello*. There were many twists and turns in our relationship. We took things slowly. We dated others. We continued to invest time in getting to know one another until a catalytic event threw us together daily.

Someone at Pop's Place, the local café, said Belinda needed a ride to work because she wrecked her car. I volunteered to take her. The world needs more Good Samaritans, I reasoned.

On the way to work that day I told Belinda my boss at Merchant's Fast Motor Freight was looking to hire a new employee. Belinda was interested. She applied the next day and got hired the day after that. Soon we were driving to work and back together every day. The regular repetition of spending time together nourished our relationship. Our relationship grew and progressed. At the end of the school year, we married.

relationships take time

I never get tired of telling that story, but there is a reason beyond the fact that I love my wife. Relationships take time. They are built experience on experience. Relationships consist of a continuum of action, thoughts, prayers, serving one another, seeing each other at the worst (not just at their best), talking through expectations, resolving hurt, forming points of view, having fun together and becoming intimate, in marriage.

God wants a relationship with you

Beginning a relationship with God is similar to the way we develop human relationships. They grow over time as we invest in them. Often we aren't looking for the relationships that become primary in our lives, just like I wasn't looking for Belinda. Although we may not be looking for a relationship with God, He is looking for us. He reveals Himself in multiple ways over time.

Open your eyes and your heart to Him and you will see that His fingerprints are everywhere. Ask Him to reveal Himself to you. Once you express a desire to Him you can be certain that He will find you. You will begin to explore what it is like to become a friend of God.

Maybe it sounds dramatic or presumptuous to imagine that you could become a friend of God. He spoke the universe into existence. He created mountains, oceans, prairies, and glaciers. He designed the ecosystems of our world. He was born into the very world He gave life. He experienced the best life had to offer and the worst. He took the sin of the world on His shoulders when He died a cruel death on the cross to satisfy the curse of sin.

This Jesus wants to be your friend. To His disciples He said, *I no longer call you servants because a servant does not know his master's business. Instead I have called you friends for everything that I learned from my father I have made known to you.*[1] When you chose to live the *SENT* lifestyle of Jesus you continue the work of the Father. Jesus sees you as a friend. Since you are a child of God you are also a brother. This is your identity. This is your destiny. Don't let anyone or anything deter you from pursuing an intimate relationship with the One who risked everything for you.

how to grow the relationship

A relationship deepens when you spend unhurried time together. It is no different in learning to relate to God. Lovers want to learn all they can about one another. Read God's Word often. Get to know Him to understand Who He is and what He desires of you.

Developing a relationship with God is similar to developing a human relationship, but there are some dramatic differences. One of the challenges of getting to know God is that you can't see Him or touch Him. It is harder to talk and listen without sensory feedback. Exercise faith and you will find that the spiritual side of your life will come alive. Value the process and give it time. The relationship you develop with God will be the most important and rewarding investment you ever make.

What began as a surprise for Belinda and me, over time, became the best human friendship of our lives. In these next chapters, I divide the idea of building a relationship with God into three sections. Love God. Love people, and live out the love of Jesus. Each one builds on the other and they culminate in describing what it means to live like Jesus. He lived SENT.

Are you ready to meet the One who wants to give you the greatest relationship possible? Do you want to deepen and expand the one you already have with Him? Whether or not you are looking for Him, He is looking for you.

a prayer for a right relationship

Lord, open my heart to the possibility of a relationship that supersedes any other. Don't let the realization that it is divine freak me out. It humbles me to think that You are seeking me out, but at the same time it gives me an incredible sense of worth. Lead me to step into the divine moment right in front of me. Amen.

surprised by love, chapter 5
questions for thought or discussion

1. What are the similarities between beginning a relationship with a person and with God?

2. What are the differences?

3. Have you begun a relationship with God?

4. What do you want to do next to help that relationship grow?

footnotes
1. John 15:5

get to know God

"Take one step toward God and He will
take two steps toward you."

—Cliff Sanders

In the movie, *Meet the Parents*, Ben Stiller offers a prayer at a family meal time that was awkward. Ben, playing the part of Greg, when he was asked to pray, didn't know what to say. He began addressing God with words outside his normal vocabulary. He used a voice different than his normal conversational tone. It was so noticeable several opened their eyes to see what changed. He soon exhausted any original thoughts, so he began to quote the words to the *Godspell* tune, *Day by day these three things I pray: to see Thee more clearly, to love Thee more dearly and to follow Thee more nearly day by day by day. Amen!*

I laugh every time I see the clip because it is so true to life. Maybe you've found yourself in the place where you want to pray but don't know how. We make it harder than it needs to be.

talking to God

Prayer at its essence is simply talking to God. You can pray aloud, under your breath, or simply by thinking thoughts in your head toward God, and He hears. Speak to Him conversationally. No special *prayer voice* is necessary.

I admit it does seem a little odd in the beginning to talk aloud to someone you can't see. To focus you may close your eyes. But remember, closing your eyes or folding your hands isn't a requirement. You have the attention of the Creator of the Universe. Know that He loves you so much He died for you and nothing pleases Him more than for you to talk to Him.

he longs to hear your voice

I'm a parent of three children and I'm also a grandparent (yes, it is as good as people say it is!) There are few things in life I value more than talking to my family. God earnestly desires to hear your prayers. Your prayers don't need to be long to impress God. He already knows the situation, and He knows you better than you know yourself. The better you know God the more you will want to set aside uninterrupted time daily to meet with Him.

in it together

What prayer does is support the reality that you and God are in this life together. He is here. You are in relationship with Him. Prayer becomes more and more like a running conversation when you make time to pause and listen.

You can pray at home in a quiet place, on a walk, while you run or bike, in a car (keep your eyes open), at work, in a time of emergency or create extended time where you may add solitude, meditation, and journaling. Include God in your everyday life, and you'll find you have a relationship moving away from ritual or routine toward love.

Jesus, when He walked the earth, often rose early in the morning to spend time alone with the Father, or He spent time late into the night. He set the example for us, and His life gave evidence of divine power as a result.

a pattern for prayer

When His disciples asked Him to teach them to pray, He gave them what we've come to call, The Lord's Prayer, found in Matthew 6. *Pray like this: Our Father in heaven, may Your name be kept holy. May Your kingdom come soon. May Your will be done on earth, as it is in heaven. Give us today the food we need, and forgive us our sins, as we have forgiven those who sin against us. And don't let us yield to temptation but rescue us from the evil one.*[1]

a pattern for prayer

I believe Jesus intended this prayer to be a pattern for daily prayer. It covers the subject matter that concerns us every day. Let's explore it further.

address

The address comes first. It is normal to address the person to whom you speak, and it is natural to praise them. Jesus says His prayer is to *His Father in heaven* and that He is *Holy*[2] (or set apart from all others). I find it helpful to start conversations or prayers with compliments. When you pray it is good to start with praise for who God is and thanks for what He has done.

mission

Next we see the motivation to live a life that is *SENT*. Jesus puts the needs of the kingdom of God first. *May Your kingdom come soon. May Your will be done on earth, as it is in heaven.* Jesus prays that what is normal in heaven becomes normal on earth. By making this the first request He reminds us of our high calling to fulfill the will of the Father—that everyone would know His love. It's always appropriate to begin our prayers by dedicating ourselves to do God's will so heaven touches earth in the world in which we live.

petition

Then Jesus acknowledges we have daily needs. He prays, *Give us today the food that we need.* Isn't it great to know that He cares about your needs? Whatever is important to you is important to Him. Nothing is too small to escape His interest, and nothing is too big for God. Ask Him for what you need or want. It blesses Him when you do. If it is important to you it is important to him.

Jesus said it like this, *Ask using my name, and you will receive, and you will have abundant joy.*[3]

healing

Then He continues with a subject matter we often like to avoid—broken relationships. Since everything is about relationships wouldn't it naturally follow to include them in our prayers daily? Jesus says to acknowledge we are prone to go our own way. Ask God to *forgive* you and in the same way offer forgiveness to others who sin against you.

victory

Conclude your prayer time by asking for victory in your spiritual life. Pray to be strong against *temptations*. I suggest you name them. And pray that God will *deliver* you from the adversary of your soul often called the devil. Ask God to show you how you can win in the most important battles of this life—the battle for your soul and the spiritual vitality of others.

not a Grocery List

Keep in mind that the greatest benefit to prayer is not necessarily the answers—it is the deepening of relationship. This will help you avoid treating prayer like a time where you bring your grocery list of needs to God. Some of the best conversations I have with my children aren't where we are simply problem solving, but they are times when we have a deepening of understanding between us. When we connect at a heart level, I feel confident that we will find the solutions needed.

dialog

We call it prayer, but at the simplest level it is about including God in your everyday life. As you grow in love it becomes more of a dialog and less of a monologue.

No wonder the Bible describes prayer like this, *Be joyful always; pray continually; give thanks in all circumstances, for this is God's will for you.*[2]

listening

And an important part of any love relationship is listening. You could make the case that listening is the best test of truly loving. When you relate to God, you will naturally want to listen. Once again we have that unique challenge since we can't see God with our eyes. God is Spirit, and we must learn to discern His leading in a spiritual way.

the Bible

Fortunately, God gave us His word in written form, and we can read it. His words were written by people but inspired by the Holy Spirit. They are recorded in the Bible, and they speak in a fresh way to us today. Take time to read it daily, and when you do, expect the Spirit of God to speak to you. I encourage you to breathe a prayer under your breath when you sit down to read the Bible that goes like this, *Holy Spirit speak to me today through your living word.*

I am continually amazed at how relevant applications and divine insight pop out to me when I read the Bible. The Holy Spirit points out what it means to me in my context and how to live it out. There is an amazing harmony between God's written word and the practical guidance given to live it. God speaks and leads. You relate to Him in by listening and following.

guidance

Once when I was struggling to discern God's leading, I thought God might be directing me to leave the church I loved and served for over seven years, the First Church of God, in Kansas City, Kansas. If I heard Him right, I concluded He wanted me to plant a new church in Olathe, Kansas. I wrestled with the idea for many reasons. I found contrasting points of view in my mind created a stalemate in decision making. I needed to hear from God.

only a shadow

I'll never forget the Wednesday night service where we took an extended time for prayer. A good friend, Jan Mathias, said she felt impressed to tell me to read Hebrews 10 when I got home. The first verse literally jumped off the page. Here's how I read it, *The old...was only a shadow, a dim preview of the good things to come.*[3] When I read it my spirit immediately felt confirmation of what I'd been suspecting, God wanted me to trust Him to leave the familiar and do something I had never done before, start a new church. That church, the Indian Creek Community Church, became the ministry I led for the next quarter of a century plus. I'm glad I listened, even though it was initially difficult to receive.

God is speaking. Are you listening?

more than reading

There are actually two different Greek words used to describe the *Word* of God. One is *logos,* and it refers to the written word or what we call the Bible. It is interesting that the Bible also uses the word *logos* to describe Jesus.[4]

The other Greek word for our English word *word,* is *rhema.* It refers to the speaking word of the Holy Spirit. They work together to make God's word come alive in your daily life.

memorize

When you commit God's word to memory, it is incredible how the Holy Spirit brings it back to your mind at just the right moment. It actually feels like you are living life in relationship with your best friend who also happens to be God.

The written word and the Spirit's speaking word are meant to fit together like a hand in a glove. If you have the written word without the spoken application from the Spirit, it is easy for the Bible to feel more like law than life. If you have feelings and applications without the written word, it is difficult to discern if they are grounded in truth. We need both the written word and the speaking word of the Spirit to get to the best decisions. This is how we share life with God who is our Friend.

S.O.A.P.

A practical way to relate to God through His Word is to use the acrostic S.O.A.P. Record your thoughts in a journal so you can keep them as a ready reference.

S Scripture Ask what does it say?

Read a chapter of the Bible, or even a paragraph or verse, slowly so you can comprehend it. Let it sink in. Roll it over several times in your mind. Read it out loud to give it priority in your thoughts. Process it until it makes sense to you.

Do this daily. It helps to have a systematic plan for reading through the scripture. If you are not sure where to begin start begin by reading a chapter a day in the Gospel of Mark. If you are ready for more options go online to www.Youversion.com and chose a reading plan that fits your needs.

I encourage you to read through the Bible annually. You can do it in 3-4 chapters a day.

O Observation Ask what does it mean?

Notice the details, like names, places, and notable events. Put them in the context of the message. Take the time to form a frame of reference in order to better understand the meaning. You can find many Bible helps online including Commentaries, Bible dictionaries, Maps, Concordances, and more.

A Application   Ask *how should I **apply** this?*

What are the obvious applications? Think general then think specific. Write down the principals. Ask God what applications are specific to you. Write down some ways you can begin to put this into practice in your everyday life.

P Prayer   Ask God *how do I **Personalize** this?*

Form the thoughts you've collected into a prayer with specific next steps. Invite the Holy Spirit to speak to you specifically. Pray for guidance so you can put the Word into practice in your life.

a prayer to know God better

God, thank You for sending Jesus, and for taking the first step to develop a loving relationship with me. I want to grow in my ability to relate to You. Help me as I pray and listen. I pray that living in love will become natural for me. And I pray it will also bring a smile to your face. Amen

get to know God, chapter 6
questions for thought or discussion

1. When and how did you come to discover that God loves you?

2. What are some ways you are learning to love Him in return?

3. How would you describe the way you relate to God in prayer?

4. In what ways would you like to grow in prayer?

5. Describe how you approach Bible reading, is it helpful to you and how?

6. What are some take-aways from today's study that would help you grow in the way you listen to God's word?

footnotes
1. Matthew 6:9-13 NLT
2. 1 Thessalonians 5:16-18 NIV
3. Hebrews 10:1
4. Matthew 6:9 NIV
5. John 16:24 NLT
6. John 1:1 NLT

lay down your cards

"The power of a consecrated life is discovered in our willingness
to be cleansed from the self life to the Christ life."
—Stan Toler

Sometimes I like to walk and pray out loud. It works well when I'm up early. If I sit still too early in the morning, I can easily fall back asleep. One day I was walking and praying in the Activity Center at Indian Creek Community Church.

I read and I prayed, *I want to know Christ and experience the mighty power that raised him from the dead.*[1] I liked the sound of that.

I said, *Yes God, I want that!* Power and miracles sounded good.

The next sentence in the scripture text read, *I want to suffer with him, sharing his death, so that one way or another I will experience the resurrection from the dead.*[2] Wait a minute! I didn't like the sound of that part of the verse nearly as well as the first part. Was it possible to have the blessing without the suffering?

Suddenly, I realized I was caught in a selfish prayer. I wanted the blessing but not the sacrifice.

The Holy Spirit spoke to me through my thoughts, *You can't have a resurrection without a death. You can't know me if you don't suffer.* I shuttered inside. This sounded ominous as if suffering was coming my way. I wondered if God was preparing me for something that would be similar to the sufferings of Christ. Was this a precursor of difficulty to come?

Was it too late to take back my prayer that I wanted to know Him at any cost? The truth was that I really did want to know Him. I didn't know what all this meant, but it was truly the desire of my heart to know God more intimately.

I can't explain what happened next with logic or with words, but I had an experience with God that I'll try to describe because I think it is helpful. God brought the story of Abraham and Isaac to my mind. You can find the story in Genesis 22.

God communicated with me that He wanted me to offer to Him that which was most dear. To identify what was most precious to me was the easy part. It was my family. Did this revelation mean I would lose another family member?

I knew too well the intense grief and pain involved in losing someone so close. I pictured my wife Belinda's face before me. I thought of Kristen, my oldest daughter. My mind turned to my two sons: Jeremy and Luke. The thought of another loss was so heavy I could hardly walk. I fell to my knees and began crying out to God to find another way.

While I was on my knees I heard these words in my spirit. *Imagine that you were playing solitaire, and all you had were face cards. I want you to place every face that is important to you in rows facing up. I can pick up any card I want and take it away from you,and your response to me is to say, "The Lord gives and the Lord takes away, blessed be the name of the Lord."*[3] This sounded ominous.

You may not be familiar with the idea that God speaks to us through our thoughts. I recognize this is very subjective, but I'm simply relating what seemed very apparent to me at the time.

When the question from God touched on everything important to me my concern broadened. Evidently what God was communicating to me included: friends, co-workers, Indian Creek, ministry in general, my home—everything! This was overwhelming! By now I was laying face down on the carpeted floor. This felt like a warning from God that I was about to have an experience like the story of Job in the Bible.[4]

There were no warm fuzzies that morning. However, there was ultimately a sense of God's presence and His peace gave me the strength to get up and go home. I knew my service to God was about to be purified. I just didn't know how. It didn't take long to find out.

I'll spare you the details, but at that time life was going splendidly well. That was about to change. Over the next several years everything important to me was tested and some disappeared from my life completely.

If I stopped the story there I would do it a gross misrepresentation. The other side of the coin was that the peace and power of God's presence became more and more real to me. I really did come to know Him in ways I never knew were possible. I'm still a work in process and this purifying work is still going on, but I wouldn't trade anything I lost for the tremendous gain of knowing Him better and becoming more like Him.

don't be afraid of God

Don't be afraid of God or anything He asks you to do. Offer to lay down the cards of your life before Him and tell Him you want to know Him whatever it takes. This is true love. This is true worship. This is what it means to live *SENT*.

This is what Jesus did. He accepted the will of the Father for His life in order to pay the price for humankind's sin. *Though He was God He did not think of equality with God as something to cling to. Instead He gave up His divine privileges; he took up the humble position of a slave and was born as a human being.*[5]

be like Jesus

I often think *I could never be like Jesus. I'll blow it for sure.* The truth is, you will. No doubt you've tried in your own strength to balance out the bad in your life with good, and you know the futility of that effort. It is very de-motivating to hear someone say that the goal of following Christ is to become like Him. I've had friends say, *I'm not going to start because I know I can't do it.*

you can't do it alone

Two things are both true: that is the goal, to become like Christ and yes, you can't do it. But Jesus can and will do it through you if you will let Him. It isn't about trying harder as much as it is about admitting you can't and asking for Him to live through you. Take heart and remember that the weight of transforming you into the likeness of Christ is on God's shoulders. He owns the responsibility of getting you to the finish line of life. Your responsibility is to cooperate with Him. He is good at what He does.

The scripture tells us, *I am certain that God, who began the good work within you, will continue his work until it is finally finished on the day when Christ Jesus returns.*[6] He doesn't say He might or maybe He will, He will! Let Him do what He wants to do in your life. He will stay after it until He comes, or you go to Him through death's door. Don't worry. You can do it! He won't give up on you and He won't quit. Don't quit on Him!

live a lifestyle of worship

This journey of becoming more like Jesus is what I calling living a life of worship. In this lifestyle everything is surrendered all the time. I need to lay the cards of my life down daily. Each time I do God does a work in me that filters out more of self.

However, the process doesn't leave me empty. The opposite is true. God fills me with His Holy Spirit. He gives me the fruit of the Spirit, *love, joy, peace, patience, kindness, goodness, faithfulness, gentleness, and self-control.* [7]These are graces from God that I don't deserve, but which God gives through the gift of His Spirit. They can be yours, too.

God is honored when we trust Him. When others know just how human and fallible I am, and yet they see God at work in me they know there must be a God! This act of surrender is to love God so much that you let Him transform you into His image. This is living a life that is *SENT.* Neither you nor I will get it perfect. And when we don't—there is grace. Your humanity surrendered to Him makes you a trophy of his grace.

treasure in jars of clay

One night my wife, Belinda, was explaining the miracle it is that a perfect God is willing to live in a fallible human on a women's retreat. She was using the scripture that says, *We have this treasure in jars of clay to show that this all-surpassing power is from*

God and not from us.[8] We, in our humanity, are like the clay pots. In Jesus' time the pots were similar to a lantern. A candle was placed inside and the light shined out the top. However, as they aged they also developed cracks in the sides. Light shined through the cracks, and in so doing it revealed that there is something greater than the darkness inside the pot. The point she wanted to make was that we have this treasure of Christ in us, and He shines out through our weaknesses. She wanted the women to embrace the truth that God desires to live in us and work through us. Our brokenness and humanity is an opportunity for Him to shine through us.

She was doing well until she simplified the message to one sentence. She said they needed to let Christ shine through their cracks. First there was a snicker or two, but she continued on oblivious to another way to think about what she was saying.

Belinda, who was very sincere about the point she made, was caught off guard. She became more emphatic, *We need to let God shine through our cracks!* The room erupted in laughter at the imagery!

Then, it dawned on her how most of the women were hearing it. She too laughed so hard she couldn't stop. Embarrassed, she turned away from the crowd to hide her face. Now they had a visual! What she did next was unbelievable but true. She was laughing so hard she thought she might lose control so she bent over. That was exhibit A of the point she tried to make! They practically fell off their seats laughing. Needless to say, it was hard to put that talk back together.

It is funny, but she did have it right! And she illustrated it without meaning to, not by bending over, but by her humanity. God can use you at your best or even with your limitations. They got the message in a way that they will never forget. And I'm guessing you won't either. When we are weak but we give Him our best, He is strong.

more than a song

Surrendering everything we have and are to God is an act of worship. All too often we've reduced the word *worship* to something we do in a gathering of Christ followers. We think of worship as a song, or a prayer or a reading of scripture. A worship service can certainly be catalytic in nature to usher us into the presence of God, but that is a by-product not the goal. The goal is to offer our best to God. When we do that privately or corporately, there is a sense of God's presence as if He's loving on us in return.

When people come to a gathering expecting to *be fed* and evaluating what takes place by how it fits their appetite for singing or teaching, they miss the point. I've heard people say they attend a gathering hoping to get enough to last them all week. A worship service is certainly a time for equipping Christ followers to live out the love of Jesus. And it is a time when those exploring can come to a place of decision. However, the weight of consumerist expectations often creates a problem.

A service intended to lead people to worship can become an exercise in pleasing the crowd or even worse, if pride gets in the way, delivering a show.

Jesus said *True worshipers must worship in spirit and truth.*[9] He spoke about a lifestyle of loving God and living for Him with both your head and your heart involved. It is not how you sing, pray, or exegete the scriptures but what is in your heart and mind that matters most. You truly worship when you live or participate in a worship gathering to give to God.

That certainly applies to a church worship service, but it applies to what we do for God outside the service, too. There are six other days in the week to worship God. For this reason, I prefer to call what we do on Sundays a *gathering* since worship is something we can do anytime anywhere.

Traditionally, we have set aside Sunday as a day to gather as a community to worship God. There are six other days and 167 other hours where we can worship. He deserves our worship 24/7. This is a much, much bigger privilege, and it shouldn't be relegated to one day, one hour a week.

you are the church

The word *church* is not the best word to describe a service either. A *church* is not a building, a program, or a gathering. A *church* is not a facility. A church is the description of the community of people who are following Jesus. He said, *Where two or three gather as my followers, I am there among them.*[10] Whenever Christ followers gather, Jesus is in the middle of whatever they are doing.

Some of the best worship takes place outside the walls of our church facilities. Is serving in your local grade school worship? Absolutely! Is it possible to worship on your job? It is if we realize that worship is offering God our best. Anywhere and anytime we give God our best we are worshipping Him. When you live for Him at work you are exercising the gifts and talents He has given to you. In this way you are continuing the witness of God in the world. You are letting Him shine through your cracks!

the incarnation

You might be the only Christ follower your co-workers know. Just like nature gives glory to God by fulfilling its' purpose you continue the mission of God when you give back to God what He's given to you.

It is in these moments of time that the life of Christ is incarnated, or we could say *comes alive*, in you. In other words, He comes alive in you, and people notice. He was already there, but He shines brightest when you release His light into a world walking in darkness.

the mission of God

In this way you continue the mission of God. It is less about launching out into something new in your life and asking God to bless you than it is in watching what God is already doing in you and letting Him have His way. When you see a place where God is already working join Him in it as His servant. This is the *Missio Dei*, a Latin phrase that literally translates *the sending of God*.

worship is giving

Loving God will cost you. It isn't that God needs what you have. It is that you need to live a lifestyle of worship. One that is so unencumbered by the things of this world that you are free to give or receive without controlling the process. That is the nature of relationships.

Many of us get stuck when it comes to giving and this is unfortunate. The reality is that we wouldn't have anything if God didn't trust it to us first. Why should we be surprised if He asks for it back? I'm convinced that when God asks us for the tithe (literally translated 10%) to be returned to Him in the local storehouse (the church) it is because He wants us to remember that it is all His in the first place. We need to live with a heart ready to give whatever He wants whenever He wants it. When we give the tithe we remember that He gave first and that He takes the responsibility of caring for His obedient children.

the fight over offerings

The history of humanity was only four chapters old when in Genesis 4 Cain and Abel got in a fight over what was appropriate to offer God! What was intended to be an act of worship turned into a jealous competition on Cain's part. He murdered his brother because he didn't understand the point of the offering. Let's look more closely at their story.

Cain brought an offering that cost him little. He took a portion of the grain he grew, and he gave it. Abel gave his best, the life of the firstborn from his flock. The grain would grow back and hardly be missed. The gift of a life surrendered was pleasing to God because it revealed complete dependence on God to provide. Once the life was lost it was gone. It would not grow back. Isn't it interesting that the one who gave the least was the same one who was the least satisfied with the result?

If you go through life trying to control people or control God through whatever way you might try, you will ultimately be miserable. Cain was competitive and suspicious even as he gave. But when you give what you have, you lay every card on the table. You will be free to live life at it's' best. God will reveal Himself through you and not only will you worship Him but your example will prompt the same in others. Nothing in this life is more fulfilling.

Jesus reoriented His disciples with these words, *If you try to hang on to your life, you will lose it. But if you give up your life for my sake and for the sake of the Good News, you will save it.*[11]

pray with me: *Lord, as hard as it is to say this, I know I need to lay down the cards of my life. I say it with my will even though my heart trembles inside of me. I want to know You. I invite You to shape me in Your image. Empty me of self and fill me with Your Spirit. Reveal Yourself to me in ever increasing ways. Thank You for the privilege of being sent to love God and live a life of worship. Amen.*

lay down your cards, chapter 7
questions for thought or discussion

1. Do you desire to know Jesus?

2. Whom or what do the cards you hold in your hand represent?

3. Which would be the hardest to lie down, and why?

4. Recall a time in your life where God led you through a loss and on the other side you were stronger? How did that happen?

5. Would you be willing to voluntarily surrender now like Jesus did in the Philippians 2?

6. What is the treasure we have in broken pots?

7. Have you ever experienced God shining through your cracks? Would you be willing to share it?

8. Are you willing to consider giving to God as an act of worship?

footnotes

1. Philippians 3:10a NLT
2. Philippians 3:10b NLT
3. Job 1:21 NLT
4. Job 1:13-21 NLT
5. Philippians 2:6, 7 NIV
6. Galatians 5:22 NLT
7. Philippians 1:6 NLT
8. 2 Corinthians 4:7 NIV
9. John 4:24 NIV
10. Matthew 18:20 NLT
11. Mark 8:35 NLT

love people

who am i?

"Very often when I have no faith in my faith, I have to
have faith in His faith. He makes me believe in myself
and my possibilities, when I simply can't."

—E. Stanley Jones

In the movie *Bourne Identity*, Jason Bourne, the lead character,
struggles to determine his true identity. He has amnesia with
flashbacks to traumatic events. He is sure they shaped his present
reality, but he can't put the pieces together. He remembers fleeing
for his life. He remembers it was kill or be killed at some point, but
why? What was the motive? Was there a purpose? And who was the
girl with him?

Jason strains to learn if there was a moral value to the
pursuit of his life. He fears he may have been a rouge on the
run perhaps even from himself. Bit by bit, piece by piece, his
memory returned, and he began to sort out who he was
separate from what he did. Once he discovered the truth, he
began to live out of his true identity. The truth was the key to

discovering his life's quest that indeed he had a higher purpose than self-preservation.

I'll stop there so I don't spoil the story, but in the same way it is critical that you and I discover our true identity. I imagine you have a head start on Jason Bourne in the condition he was in, but no doubt you feel the struggle inside to determine who you are at the core. It is normal to want to discover why you do what you do. You desperately hope that there is a higher purpose and a moral value that drives you forward. Surely there is a grand reason you are alive.

At the same time there is innate good in you, there likely are base desires that scare you with their intensity. Where do they come from? What feeds them? How do you escape the inevitable selfishness that threatens to consume you? Why does the path of least resistance usually lead you to a place of shame? Are you defined by what you do? Or is there more inside you?

What if you could harness the drive and passion that is inborn away from selfishness into alignment with your life's purpose? The key is to discover your true identity. To find the truth you must be willing to search.

the search for truth

Clandestine meetings aren't only a part of the plot of a thriller movie, but they are a part of a bigger quest that goes on in the soul of a person on a spiritual journey toward truth. The Bible tells the story of a man named Nicodemus who sought out Jesus at night because he didn't want to be seen with him in the day. Let's give him an up-to-date name like Nick. Clearly Nick was curious about who Jesus was. And if Jesus had a message from God, it would help him sort out the question of his own life.

The conversation between the two became a classic dialog for spiritual formation. Nick launched the discussion with a statement that implied there was a greater question. It appeared that God was working through the man called Jesus, but who was he really? Was he the Messiah, the one the Jews expected would be the long anticipated Savior? Nick danced around the question as he spoke to Jesus without directly asking.

Jesus flipped the conversation and talked about how it was that Nicodemus would discover spiritual truth in the first place. In other words, it wasn't Jesus who was on trial here. Nick needed to question whether he correctly knew how to discern truth. The implied question in the words of Jesus was whether or not Nick really knew for what he was searching. To understand his own purpose in the conversation Nick was going to need to come face to face with his spiritual side of life. Jesus said he needed to be "born again."

Now there was a man of the Pharisees named Nicodemus, a member of the Jewish ruling council. He came to Jesus at night and said, "Rabbi, we know you are a teacher who has come from God. For no one could perform the miraculous signs you are doing if God were not with him."

In reply, Jesus declared, "I tell you the truth; no one can see the kingdom of God unless he is born again."

"How can a man be born when he is old?" Nicodemus asked. "Surely he cannot enter a second time into his mother's womb to be born!"

Jesus answered, "I tell you the truth, no one can enter the kingdom of God unless he is born of water and the Spirit."[1]

This conversation concerned spiritual concepts, and it quickly went deep. Nicodemus evidenced his shallow fleshly thinking when he wondered aloud how a man could enter the womb a second time. Jesus' answer was profound. He spoke of a duality of life where the physical nature of life coexists with a spiritual side. There is a powerful purpose that comes alive inside when you discover that your body and soul are meant to align your Creation's plan. This discovery is a powerful clue to sorting out your true identity and living out your destiny. You too must learn the lesson Jesus taught Nicodemus.

my story

I find it easy to determine my human heritage. I am the son of Paul and Ruthie Kendall. I grew up in Alaska where my parents were on assignment as missionaries in the Church of God, Anderson, IN. I have a brother named Brad who is four years younger. I married Belinda Barker Kendall in 1979 and we have four children Kristen, Jeremy, Luke and Megan. That is the skinny on me.

There is much more to me, of course, than just my physical lineage. I could tell you what I do, but even then I am more than a human-doing. I'm a human-being complete with a spiritual nature. There are passions inside me for justice and mercy. I'm sure they are God given. Just as certainly there are selfish desires that I want and need to keep in check. Where do they come from? Who am I really?

your story

You too are born of flesh. You have human parents. You have the DNA and heritage they gave you. On top of that, you made choices of your own that brought you to where you are today. Surely you've reflected on those noting that at times you were proud of the inner drive and passion. It is just as true that there are things you wouldn't want others to know. Most people have a fair amount of shame inside related to the times selfishness won the day.

So here is the question: who are you? Are you innately good or you inherently flawed? Are you a mixture of both? If so is that by design? Whose design is it? And what do you do about the tug-of-war that goes on in your soul? You are drawn toward good because you were created in the image of God. You are drawn toward sin because...well, why is that?

Jesus unlocked the code for us. He told Nick that everyone is born into the world through a physical birth and that made him human. He had fleshly desires that were natural. Jesus didn't say it here, but the Bible tells us, that we are all born with a bent to sin due to Adam's original sin. However, as Jesus told Nick, there was a spiritual rebirth possible that could redeem and transform his soul. It is the longing to reconnect with God that drew Nick to Jesus in the first place. Nick had a God shaped hole in his soul. That is what drew him to Jesus.

These things are spiritually discerned and Nick struggled to grasp them. It is entirely possible that this might be a new concept for you, too. You are not alone. In Jesus' explanation he gave us a valuable piece of the puzzle in putting the picture of our life together. We must believe in God's love for us. It started before we were conceived. There is a plan greater than we know at work. It was a life giving plan of redemption.

Jesus' story

Jesus used his own life as an illustration for Nick to understand his life purpose. Jesus knew his own identity. He spoke with confidence about who he was and why he was here on earth. He lived to die. He was sent on a rescue mission to save Nick, to save you and everyone else who would believe in his love.

Jesus died on the cross to pay for your sin and the sin of every other person who would ever life. The story Jesus told of the snake being lifted up in the desert illustrated that Jesus knew he was born to offer his life in a substitutional manner.

"No one has ever gone into heaven except the one who came from heaven—the Son of Man. Just as Moses lifted up the snake in the desert, so the Son Man must be lifted up, that everyone who believes in him may have eternal life. For God so loved the world that he gave his one and only Son, that whoever believes in him shall not perish but have eternal life."[2]

the sin virus

Sin entered the world like a virus through the choice of one man, Adam. Jesus was just one man, but he came to earth bringing the antidote in his blood. Here is how that worked. Jesus was born fully God, but born of a virgin, so he was also human. Jesus' choice was to live inside of the will and power of the Father and Spirit, so he was the only man to ever live without sin. He lived the life he lived, not through the strength of his divinity, but through his reliance on the will of the Father and Spirit. In that way, he was like anyone of us—human and drawn to sin by his flesh.

Jesus was put to death by the Romans because he claimed to be God. He came to die as a sacrifice, taking on himself the sin of the world. He paid for your sin and my sin with his life. He was an appropriate sacrifice for the sin of the world because he was sinless. Sin entered the world through one man, Adam, and forgiveness would come through one man, Jesus.

be your own god

Adam made the claim to be his own god when he chose against God's will. Jesus was put to death for claiming to be God. Jesus was condemned and sentenced to death because he claimed to be

God. It wasn't his sin because his claim was true. Clearly he died for Adam's sin and for anyone else who commits the sin of trying to be their own god.

I've done that when I chose my way over God's way. At some point, you, like every other person, made the claim to be your own god. You've chosen against your conscious, the image of God in you, and you too fell short of God's plan. But Jesus had good news for Nick, and he has good news for me and for you.

your choice

Now you get a second chance. You get to choose whether you will do life on your own. Will you try desperately and ineffectively to manage the good and sinful desires in you? Or will you accept the forgiveness purchased for you? What you decide determines whether you discover your true identity or live out of a pseudo self that tries to make life work on your own.

Jesus concluded the secret meeting with Nick by giving a word of warning. Jesus came not to judge nor condemn Nick for the fact that he had the sin virus alive inside but to save him from it. He provided the anti-virus with his own God/man blood. But Nick and everyone else must choose to either identify with Christ or go it alone. Everyone makes this choice. Not to decide is to decide to go your own way—that choice places you in the path of God's judgment against sin.

For God did not send his Son into the world to condemn the world, but to save the world through him. Whoever believes in him is not condemned, but whoever does not believe stands condemned already because he has not believed in the name of God's one and only Son."[3]

We have no record here of what Nick decided. There is no mention of him for many chapters in the story of Jesus, as told by John, until much later. I wonder if Nick remembered Jesus words about being lifted up to die a sacrificial death. Because ironically, it was after the death of Jesus on the cross, that Nick was the one who stepped up and took the risk to identify with Jesus when he offered to take charge of Jesus' dead body. Evidently Nick discovered the truth of Who Jesus was, and in the process, he discovered his own identity in Him.

This is how one discovers your true identity. When you believe Jesus is the Son of God and that He died for you, there is a spiritual rebirth inside of you. You are reborn to the DNA of God placed in you from creation forward. Until that moment, it was latent but waiting to explode with passion, godly desire, purity and purpose. It is remarkable that there is a whole side of you ready to truly live. You were made for this! You were made for more than serving self.

a divine destiny

You have a divine destiny waiting for you. You were designed by the Master, spiritually engineered to live *SENT* by God as an agent of redemption. God wants you to know your true self. Your soul can be united into one integrated, whole person. This is your spiritual identity. It is time you discovered it. And in an amazing turn of events God wants to use you to help others find life in Jesus.

your family

When you believe you are adopted into the family of God. Ironically, this was always your family, but you disconnected outside of Jesus. When you go your own way you are on your own. When you accept Jesus you came home to your original family where you belong.

"*To all who received him, to those who believed in his name, he gave the right to become children of God—children born not of natural descent, nor of human decision of a husband's will, but born of God.*"[4]

your rights and privileges

There are rights and privileges that are yours as a child of God. This is incredible but true! You receive the very righteousness of Christ in you. Previously when God looked at you, He saw the true you, but your sin separated you from Him. Once you laid down your way and choose Jesus, God looks at you and sees the person you were always made to be. And, here is the impressive part, He sees the Spirit of Jesus, the Holy Spirit, inside of you!

He no longer sees your sin. It is forever forgiven and forgotten. He looks at you and sees the unobscured image of His Son in you. You are spiritually aligned with God and a part of God's forever family. This is God's grace at work! As a family member, you have new rights and privileges. Everything the Father has is now yours. You are a part of His inheritance. There are some three hundred plus promise of God, and they are rightfully yours. You can claim them and live out of their truth. Of course, you need to know the benefits to take advantage of this new life. We will talk a lot more about that as we journey on this path of spiritual growth.

your enemy

You may be just now learning the value of your right standing with God not being rooted in the amount of good you've done. But you already have an enemy. There is someone else in the picture who wants you continually confused about your identity ,and that is our enemy Satan. He was in the garden tempting Adam and Eve, and he will be on your doorstep, too. When you realize that your ability to be in a right relationship with God is based on what Jesus did for you and your acceptance of His gracious gift, Satan can't hold your sin over your head.

That won't stop him from lying to you about who you really are. Prepare yourself by rehearsing the truth of scripture again and again until is unshakeable. Then you can stand up to the deceiver and claim your identity is with Christ. Tell the defeated enemy to leave you alone and take a hike back to where he belongs. The Bible says you are seated with Christ in positional authority over your spiritual enemy, and you have every right to command him to leave you alone, in Jesus' name. He must go! You don't have to listen to his shame. You can bind his activity against you through prayer and the scripture. When you take your authority over him the devil loses, and you are free.

"Truly I tell you, whatever you bind on earth will be[a] *bound in heaven, and whatever you loose on earth will be*[b] *loosed in heaven.*[5] Matthew 18:18 NIV

You are saved, not by your righteous works, but by Jesus' gift of forgiveness. Even your failures become trophies of God's grace. You were created to live in victory. You are a child of the most High God. You are reigning with Him even now while you live on earth. The life of Christ will continue to grow in you as you let the Holy Spirit lead and you obey. He will form the person of Jesus inside you daily if you cooperate. All that is in the kingdom of heaven is yours. The transformation is always in process and never complete on this side of eternity. The Holy Spirit promises to fill in the gaps and grow you up in Christ who is your true identity.

baptism

A catalyst for spiritual growth is baptism. Jesus was baptized at the beginning of his ministry. It was a sign of His dedication to do the will of the Father. He set the example for us, and it is a huge statement of identification with Jesus when you do what He did. Baptism doesn't save you. But baptism is an act of obedience whereby you symbolize that you identify with Jesus' death. In baptism, you allow yourself to be laid into the water. When you go under it is as if you've entered a watery grave. You die to self. Then when you are raised out of the water, it symbolizes the new birth with Christ Jesus. You are raised to new life!

The apostle Peter speaking in Jerusalem on the day of Pentecost relayed God's will for each of us with these words.

Peter replied, "Repent and be baptized, every one of you, in the name of Jesus Christ for the forgiveness of your sins. And you will receive the gift of the Holy Spirit.[6] Acts 2:38 NIV

There is a great joy in obedience. It is always a boost to your spiritual growth to live the life Jesus lived and follow his example. Listen to the joy expressed in these quotes from people who've repented and been baptized.

I would say that getting baptized was one of most awesome things of my life. There is no greater feeling than going under the water as the old Joel and coming out of the water a renewed Joel. I personally felt Jesus touch me and refresh my body while I was under the water. Joel Johnson

The meaning of baptism for me was just incredible. It was a beautiful and an extraordinary experience. I felt the power of GOD with me in that moment. After being immersed in the water, it was as if I was breaking free, which represented a new beginning. This beginning has put me on the path where I am opening up so much in my love for Christ and his love for me. I genuinely loved the experience of declaring my faith and commitment to Jesus publicly. Jennifer Creason

My baptism symbolized my desire to be fully connected to my heavenly father GOD. In it I felt like I was dying to self and becoming fully engaged in my ever-growing, ever-lasting relationship with my best friend, Jesus. Pam Meas

I was baptized in Alaska where I lived from six years old to year sixteen. My dominate memory of that day was that it was in the winter, and there was no heater in the pool. It took my breath away! Shocking is the word that comes to my mind, but it was so worth it! There was an exhilaration that went far beyond the circumstances, and the memory is etched in my mind forever. It is one of my fondest memories to this day!

reclaim your spiritual birthright

I can't prove it to you physically, because baptism is a spiritual activity, but there is a joy and a power that is released in obedience. If you have not been baptized tell your spiritual mentor, or a pastor, you want to be baptized. Ask the person who's been the greatest spiritual motivator to you to participate and be with you in the water. Reclaim your spiritual birthright by accepting Christ. Demonstrate your change of heart by being baptized.

Baptism is a great opportunity to declare your faith choice to others. It is a way of saying to yourself, to God and to others you are "all in!" Certainly there is some trepidation for most about being laid into the water. It is humbling, and you have to exercise trust, but this is part of what makes it a catalyst for growth!

People often ask, *when should I be baptized?* I think as soon as you can once you've made the choice to follow Christ, and you understand what you are saying when you choose baptism. It could be the same day you choose Christ as your Savior and Leader. It is also true that in the early church, people dedicated themselves to fully grasp what it meant to be identified with Christ before they were baptized. It needs to be a personal choice. If you have questions, take them to a trusted spiritual mentor or a pastor, and ask them to help you study the scriptures. Pray to discern the appropriate timing. Listen for God's prompting.

love others⁰

It is natural that you would want to share this celebration with your church family. You now have spiritual brothers and sisters. You are loved and adopted. You are home in the family of God. It is also important to invite your friends, your family, your neighbors and co-workers to share this day. It is a great witness to all. In it you make an obvious choice to define who you are in Jesus. Your example may be motivating to others to pursue their own spiritual search for identity.

let's pray

Jesus, today I seek after you. I want to identify with you and find my true identity in you. Thank you for dying on the cross for my sin. Forgive me and extend your grace to me. I want to join your forever family. Thanks for adopting me and giving me all your rights and privileges. Give me the courage to stand against the enemy's lies. Show me when to be baptized, so I can follow your example. Thank you. Amen

who am i?, chapter 8
Questions for Thought and Discussion

1. Do you feel the tension between the image of God created in you and the selfishness of your fleshly desires? How do you deal with it?

2. The first topic of conversation between Nick and Jesus was about Jesus' miracles. Do you think there was more on his mind? What do you think drove him to question Jesus?

3. Read the story of the *snake in the wilderness* in Numbers 21:4-9. How did that story illustrate what Jesus came to do?

4. Does the substitutional death of Jesus make sense to you? How or why not?

5. Do you believe Jesus died for you? Have you accepted his offer of grace and forgiveness?

6. Have you followed the example of Jesus to be baptized? If not are you willing to do so? When will you take action?

footnotes
1. John 3:1-5 NIV
2. John 3:13-16 NIV
3. John 3:17-21 NIV
4. John 1:11-13 NIV
5. Matthew 18:18 NIV
6. Acts 2:38 NIV

not alone!

"We will have to repent in this generation not merely for the vitriolic words and actions of the bad people, but for the appalling silence of the good people."

–Martin Luther King, Jr.

I took my son, Jeremy, and his son, Landon, to the Lenexa, Kansas, BBQ cook-off. We joined my neighbors, Harry and Doug, who were competing. They had a tent where many of us gathered to cheer them on and of course eat their food! I ran into Chelsea there. At the time, Chelsea was just a year out of Pittsburg State University. She's a social worker. She is a young adult who is not married. She'd been attending Indian Creek for the previous two years. She had made a commitment to follow Christ and was baptized last year. With her eyes wide she pulled me off to one side and said, *I can't believe what happened at my community group last night!*

She proceeded to tell me she had gone to her group with a bit of an attitude because things hadn't been going smoothly for her lately. She was frustrated with God and had some doubts about whether He cared about what she cared about. She was amazed that when she shared openly with the group, they listened and took her doubts to heart. They connected with her at a soul level. They discussed her concerns with honesty and to them there were no dumb questions. She found some answers that night, and she learned that her group was there for her. That was encouraging, but it was just the beginning of the story.

Something else happened in the group that was a completely new experience for her. When the group got ready to pray they divided into two groups: one made up of guys and one made up of girls. The girls went downstairs for some privacy. One of the young women spoke directly to Chelsea, shared a scripture with her, and challenged her to step up to a new level of faith. As that was happening Chelsea said she heard God speak clearly to her spirit and give her exactly what she needed to hear. With tears in her eyes, Chelsea said, *I've never had that happen to me. It was awesome!*

But there was more! A young woman in the group broke down and began to cry. Curious and wanting to be supportive the other ladies gathered around her. Encouraged by their support, she shared a financial need she'd been trying to keep a secret. She and her husband were going to be evicted from their apartment if they didn't come up with the $1,000 rent within a day. They didn't have the resources to do it, and they didn't have a place to go. They weren't sure where to turn, so they had turned to their group.

Has your husband shared this with the guys? One of the young women asked. *No, we are embarrassed,* was the answer. Someone I, the group spoke up, *We will pray, but we need to talk about this as a group and pray for both of you.* And they did. But they didn't stop there.

Chelsea could hardly talk now because she started to cry which brought tears to my eyes as I listened. The ladies opened their purses and started to pool their money. They went upstairs and talked about it as a group. The guys participated, too. However, they came up short of collecting the full $1,000 needed.

The group decided to go to the closest ATM together. There they withdrew money until they had enough to cover the rent. They gave it to the grateful couple. Then to celebrate they went out to eat ice cream together and had a great time! *I've never experienced anything like that!* Chelsea said.

That BBQ tent became holy ground for a moment as Chelsea and I hugged and thanked God for the love that is present when His people gather. That is community at its best!

never alone

When you live *SENT* you are never alone. That community group loved God as they studied and prayed. That's true worship! They heard from God through the scriptures and prayer. They loved each other by listening and speaking the truth in love. Then they lived out their faith by giving sacrificially without judgment. God was honored, and their lives witnessed to the love of Jesus and His followers.

There is community for you too when you connect into the body of Christ which is the Church. A year ago Chelsea didn't know that it even existed, but now she's committed to living in community. She wouldn't think of doing life alone!

God never intended any of us to be an island to ourselves. You don't have to do life alone. You might be single for a season in life, but God promises you are never alone. If you've found your way back to God, He is with you in Spirit living inside you. *Jesus promised, I am with you always, even to the end of the world.*[1]

But there is more! Everyone who follows Christ becomes a child of God, so you are family with others who comprise what the Bible calls the *body of Christ.* You are a part of a huge global family! Commenting on this, the Apostle Paul said, *All of you are Christ's body, and each of you is a part of it.*[2] And this body is not limited by genetics, geographical locations, age, gender, or political parties!

the community within the trinity

It has always been God's plan for you to live your life in community. I say that with confidence because that is the way God's chosen to live. From eternity, God has existed as three persons in one, Father, Son, and Spirit. Together, as One, we identify them as the Trinity. They are equal and in essence One, but they are also distinct in their individual functions.

There are many evidences of the Trinity at work in the scriptures. From the beginning,[3] we find the Father creating heaven and earth. When he created, he did so by speaking the Word. Jesus is the Word that became flesh. At the same time the Holy Spirit was moving with the creation. In the Bible, the four gospels: Matthew, Mark, Luke and John, give us multiple examples of how Jesus interacted with the Father and the Spirit.

One of my favorite examples is at Jesus' baptism when the Father spoke from heaven declaring, *You are my dearly loved Son, and You bring me great joy.*[4] And at that moment, the heavens opened, and the *Spirit descended on Him like a dove*[5] All three members of the Trinity shared community in that moment. Living life in community is God's plan from the beginning for the Trinity, as well as for you and for me.

It is interesting to me that even the Ten Commandments reveal the need to be rightly connected with God and with others. The first five describe how to live in relationship with God, and the second five deal with how to get along with others.[6] The implication is that if you want to be right with God, you need to live in appropriate relationship with others. This is community.

the family as community

The family unit is another example of community, and for most of us, it is our first experience with life in community. We are born into it. The similarity of the Father, Spirit, and Son shouldn't be lost on us when we see God's original design of father, mother and child. I know there is a lot of brokenness and pain in many families today. I've experienced that in my life and family. At the same time, it is a comfort to know that God's plan was for you to be included in family. Even if you don't find community in your family of origin, He designed a forever family, which is the church, for you if you follow Him.

I encourage you; don't give up on your earthly family! You have the Trinity's help to apply divine strength, forgiveness, and grace. You may need to be the one to bring the power of God to your family. Let God will use you to make a difference.

It is His desire that families be united, redeemed, and restored. He practices community in His family and He is able to send you into your family as a person of peace to bring his light, love and truth. It is reality that others make their own choices, but never quit contending for God's best in your family. You were designed for community at home, and it is worth your undying effort.

marianne and rick

One Sunday, as I was leaving the gathering at Indian Creek, I ran into Marianne. I asked her how she was doing, and she said, *Okay.* But the look on her face said something different. I asked another question or two, and she began to cry. She told me that her husband Rick had left her. He was hooked on drugs, and she was losing hope. Outside the church facility with people walking by as we talked wasn't the time or place to counsel. I'm not a counselor anyway, so I did what any follower of Christ could do. I asked her if we could hold hands and pray. I prayed with faith believing that God had something better for the both of them.

A few days later, in the middle of the afternoon, I received a visit from Rick, her husband. I'd never met him before, and the last I knew he was living in Dallas. This was a surprise!

He asked if he could talk, and I said of course. He told me about the life he was living and how it was distasteful to him. It was killing him and destroying his family. He'd come to a moment of clarity, and he wanted to make a change. He wanted to find his way back to God. He also wanted to reconcile with Marianne.

Let's connect into a right relationship with Jesus first so He can apply His divine power to set you free from your sin and the drugs, I suggested.

Jesus said, *If the Son sets you free you are truly free.*[7]

We prayed. I could sense Rick's sincerity. I felt God's presence, and I knew God was on the move in his life.

God miraculously restored that family! Rick followed the counsel of God's Word and the leading of the Spirit and soon was sober. Years later, Rick's become a close friend and an Elder at Indian Creek. Any time I need a reminder of the power of God and the privilege He's given us in prayer, I think of Rick and Marianne.

faith at home

Live out your faith at home. The home is a natural place and the first place to practice living the *SENT* life. Read the scriptures, memorize them, pray, sing, praise God by telling stories of His work in your life. Practice hospitality by sharing community with your neighbors; share your faith with friends in your home, and go outside to serve others.

the body is there for you

The body of Christ is there for you as an extended family. It is meant to strengthen you and support throughout your life's journey. Expect it. Look for it. Provide it for others. Many times the community of Christ has kept a person on their feet. Jesus knows the heartache of broken families, and that is why he admits, *Anyone who does God's will is my brother and sister and mother.*[8]

the Inner Circle

Think of a series of circles that begins small but reaches further with each new circle. The starting place is your community with God. The next circle is your family of origin or your present family. The next is an inner circle of close friends and mentors. Even Jesus had an inner circle of three, Peter, James, and John, that shared life with Him in some of His most intimate moments.

It is important to seek out community. This is a time when many fathers are absent, when many marriages have dissolved, when people move every three years on the average. We all need community. You need an inner circle. An inner circle might look like a life-long friend or two, a mentor, a work associate, or a person from a different generation.

my accountability group

Years ago I knew I needed an inner circle, after my wife and family, in Kansas City where I could be honest with my hopes, hurts, and relationships. I was looking to participate in a group of three or four at the most where we could know each other's back stories. I wanted to be able to share life, to laugh, to be vulnerable, and to have someone know the inner struggles everyone has. I invited accountability and knew intuitively that if I didn't find it for real, I would likely seek it out in places or with persons who weren't the best. I'm privileged to walk with a small group of men who know the good, the bad, and the ugly about me and love me anyway. We remind each other from time to time we are growing old together. I want that for you, too.

a community group

The next ring in the concentric circles is a community group where you share life together. A community group takes a form similar to how an extended family operated in a different age in American life. They share life, they care for one another's needs, they pray for each other, they support each other, and cheer each other on in life. Who doesn't need that!

Sometimes this looks like a group which meets in a home, but it can also be a group of mothers who talk in a circle while their preschool children play. The lunchroom at work or a restaurant serves as a place where people meet on their Noon break from work. Serving is another thing that brings a group together.

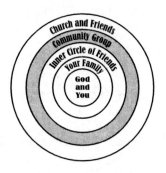

A community group functions best when it is ten or more and less than twenty. If it is smaller than ten it easily becomes exclusive and ingrown. If it is more than twenty it becomes difficult for everyone in the group to participate in the conversations. Since this is true, groups will want to work to develop new leaders continually so groups can grow, multiply, and create new groups. New groups need to be continually created so that new people coming in can also find community.

It is important to remember that as great as a community group is, it can't be everything to everyone. For that we need a growing, real relationship with Christ, a family, an inner circle, and a vital connection with the greater body of Christ. You may not have all of these working flawlessly at any one time, but living in community in the various circles will provide you sweet community through the seasons of your life. One of the writers in the Bible, Solomon, said in the scriptures, *One who has unreliable friends comes to ruin, but there is a friend who sticks closer than a brother.*[9]

dave and lisa cox

Dave and Lisa were new attendees to Indian Creek Community Church, and they didn't have any family in town. Dave played bass on the worship team, and the group developed a sense of community. Dave even overhauled a trailer to haul worship supplies back and forth from the school we rented for our gatherings.

One summer when Dave and Lisa went on a camping trip to a remote area where they were out of contact, unbeknownst to them, a pipe burst in their bathroom. Water flooded the upstairs running even down into the lower level, out the garage, and down the driveway. Their neighbors didn't know how to reach Dave and Lisa, but they remembered they had seen the Indian Creek logo and phone on their trailer which was parked on one side of the driveway. The neighbors called the church office to report the trouble. No one had a number for Dave and Lisa. However, a couple of the vocalists in the worship band, Margaret Outler and DeAnna Murguia, decided to investigate and see if there was anything they could do for their friends. When they got there they saw water damage.

When they arrived at the Cox' home, they noticed the water spilling down the driveway. At the bottom of the garage door was a small doggy door. Was it large enough for someone to crawl through to the inside? De and Margaret decided to try. To do so they would have to crawl through the water. What if they got stuck? Would the neighbors think they were breaking in? They assessed the situation and acknowledged the questions and decided to take the risk.

They made it in! They were wet, but they were inside. They found the problem. The toilet was overflowing. They shut it off. They wondered if they could find the name and number of their insurance adjuster. They didn't want mold to set in before Dave and Lisa returned. Since no one had a number for them, if they didn't start before they were scheduled to return it would be too late.

Margaret and De Anna took the liberty to look on the top of Dave's desk. After all, the Bible says to *do to others as you would have them do for you*,[11] and they would want this kind of help. They found the number for the insurance adjuster!

The adjuster came out right away and before Dave and Lisa even returned home the repair was underway. They were pleased that Margaret and DeAnna took the initiative. That incident gave them a sense of belonging in the group and in the church. This is an example of the body being the body! This is what community does. You need it, and your community needs you.

where truth and life meet

Community groups are the context in which God's Word comes to life. It is where the scriptures and life meet. They care for one another, they study and apply the scriptures, they find ways to have fun together, and they pick projects where they can serve together. We will talk more about that in the next chapters.

be a friend

Remember and practice the old adage, *To have a friend you must be a friend.* Don't wait for people to come to you and serve you. Take the first step to reach out to others. Make it your goal to leave a deposit of love in every person you meet, and you will find that you reap what you sow. What you give to others will come back to you multiplied several times over. *The farmer who plants only a few seeds will get a small crop. But the one who plants generously will get a generous crop.*[10]

a prayer for community

Lord, There are times when I think I might need to go it alone. Thanks for the reminder that You see, You know, and You share life with me. I'm never truly alone even if I feel lonely at times. Thank You that You've provided community in human ways through families and in divine ways through the Body of Christ. I pray that I will be community for others and live in community as long as I live. Amen

not alone, chapter 9
questions for thought or discussion

1. How do you picture God?

   Is He alone? If not whom else is in the picture?

2. Do you see the Trinity revealed in scripture?

3. Can you picture the Trinity at work in your life? What does it look like?

4. Do you prioritize community? What does that look like for you?

5. Who do you know that needs your friendship and inclusion in community?

footnotes

1. Matthew 28:20 KJV
2. 1 Corinthians 12:27 NLT
3. Genesis 1:1,2 NIV
4. Mark 1:11 NLT
5. Mark 1:10 NLT
6. Exodus 20:1-17
7. John 8:36 NLT
8. Mark 3:35 NLT
9. Proverbs 18:24 NLT
10. Luke 6:31 NIV
11. 2 Corinthians 9:6 NLT

redeemed

"The most difficult thing is the decision to act.
The rest is tenacity."

—Robyn Davidson

Kelly was a hurting teenager who managed to find trouble at every turn. He had a quick temper and a smart mouth. It often got him in trouble. He was a small guy in stature, and he was defensive about his size and everything else for that matter. Sports were a natural way to act out his aggression. He played baseball, basketball and football from age 7–14. But in 9th grade dropped out of every sport and became a blackout drinker. He often smoked marijuana before going to school. In 10th grade he started wrestling. It gave him the opportunity to hurt his opponent which, as he tells the story, was a good way to deal with the pain life handed him. He struggled in school and his teachers assumed he was intellectually slow. Relationships were hot and cold for him. Few things in his life seemed to be trending up and to the right for him.

No one invested in Kelly in a positive way, but there was a wrestling coach who saw through the way Kelly acted out. He saw a guy with talent, a quick wit, and a tender heart. Kelly was a good athlete and the team needed him, so the coach had extra motivation.

Over time, the trend downward continued. Kelly was kicked out of school several times for fighting which kept him on the border line of being a drop out. Kelly was raised by his dad and my granny. His Dad worked hard but then spent a lot of time at the bar after work. He went to Kelly's games but stayed outside the gate so he could drink. The coach decided it was time to step up and call Kelly out on the choices he made. Sometimes, Kelly came around and made progress. Other times, he stayed on the fringes. Consistency wasn't his strong suit.

Kelly had as many losses as wins on his record not just in athletics but in life, but he kept showing up. During this time there was one man who was as consistent as Kelly was inconsistent. He invested in Kelly repeatedly and made multiple invitations for Kelly to attend his church. Over time Kelly opened his heart to him. Because of the investment, he eventually sad yes. This guy wasn't put off by the bravado coming from Kelly's words. He saw through the act. He knew what Kelly really needed was a relationship with His heavenly Father. More than anything, he needed to find his way back to God, but he also needed positive role models. Once Kelly accepted the invitation to church and to a couple of campus Organizations he met a whole group of students.

Through the influence of these key people who took an interest in him and a set of circumstances that only the Holy Spirit could arrange, Kelly reached out to Jesus. He started by asking Him to forgive him and lead his life.

The change was dramatic. Kelly knew real love for the first time. He quickly found freedom from shame, drugs, and alcohol. His relationships improved. Now there was a whole group of Christian college students who were also seeking spiritually around him. Kelly felt hope for the first time in a long time.

Kelly married Polly, a cheerleader and one of the co-eds in the group. For the first time in his life, Kelly explored the scriptures. He found a good church. He discovered he was a leader and a gifted one at that! He started reaching out to others like a few men reached out to him. His story connected with others, and before long Kelly was leading others to find the life he found in Jesus. And in the process Kelly was becoming more and more like Jesus.

Today Kelly is a dynamic pastor who started a church House of Joy from a very small group, mostly his own family, in Valdosta, GA. The fledgling church has grown to 300 plus in five short years and shows no signs of slowing down. You would never guess that would have been his future had you met Kelly in his teen years! If you'd told Kelly what the future held for him he would have laughed at the idea.

what happened?

What happened? How did Kelly achieve such an abrupt turn-around? For one thing, he learned the truth about who he was and why he was here. Jesus came to redeem us from self destruction. Jesus said, *The Spirit...has anointed me to preach good news to the poor. He has sent me to proclaim freedom for the prisoners and recovery of sight for the blind, to release the oppressed, to proclaim...the Lord's favor.*[1]

Jesus takes our mess and makes it a masterpiece. He doesn't just forgive us; He restores the very image of God in us. He wants to do that in you. That's the first part, but there is more!

God gave Kelly spiritual gifts that are divine graces. In other words, he didn't earn or deserve them. When Kelly answered the invitation of Jesus to follow Him, the gifts came alive inside him. Kelly's story drew others to Christ. Lives were impacted, and destinies were changed.

You too can experience the life changing power of Jesus. It will be good for you. You will have your own turn-around story. It doesn't have to stop with you—your story will speak to others. What a privilege to be a partner with God in the grand story of redemption.

you have one or more spiritual gifts

Everyone who decides to let Jesus lead their life has one or more spiritual gifts. It is a grace of God in you that may or may not track along with your natural talents. It is not based on what you've done, who you are, or what you have to offer God. Spiritual gifts are supernatural endowments given to equip you to do the will of God for your life. They are intended to supersede your own abilities, and in doing so they point to God. They give Him glory for what happens in and through you. Often God chooses the most unlikely and most unsuspecting persons for roles they would never imagine. In this way, He knows they are then more likely to depend on Him.

What are the various gifts? Many are mentioned in the Bible. One list is included here: *We have different gifts, according to the grace given to each of us. If your gift is prophesying, then prophesy in accordance with your faith; if it is serving, then serve; if it is teaching, then teach; if it is to encourage, then give encouragement; if it is giving, then give generously; if it is to lead, do it diligently; if it is to show mercy, do it cheerfully.*[2]

Another section of the Bible adds to the previous list, *Now to each one the manifestation of the Spirit is given for the common good. To one there is given through the Spirit a message of wisdom, to another a message of knowledge by means of the same Spirit, to another faith by the same Spirit, to another gifts of healing by that one Spirit, to another miraculous powers, to another prophecy, to another distinguishing between spirits, to another speaking in different kinds of tongues, and to still another the interpretation of tongues. All these are the work of one and the same Spirit, and he distributes them to each one, just as he determines.*[3]

Here are some takeaways. There is level ground at the foot of the cross. No one gets a running start. We come to God not on the basis of what we do for Him but what He's done for us. And continuing in that mode, He prepares us for living a life that is *SENT* with unmerited favor. He equips every follower with one or more spiritual gifts. They are given to young and old, both genders indiscriminant of socio-economic factors or culture. This is a divine partnership between you and God.

You are gifted! God uniquely and supernaturally equipped you to fulfill a role in His grand plan of redeeming the world. God invested in you. There is something you are called to do that if you don't do it—there is a void. God trusts you, and a part of His redemptive plan depends on you.

examples

Chester Meeks is a Montana mountain man who is most comfortable with an axe in his hand to chop wood or a rifle to shoot game. But when he begins to share Christ with people, there is a supernatural gifting that opens hearts. Fred Hale is a farmer who has the gift of faith. If you need someone to pray for you, find Fred. Enrique Cepeda gushes encouragement. He makes you feel like a million bucks in the first five minutes you are around him. No wonder God's used him to prepare many Christ followers to be at their best as businessmen in the marketplace. Jeremy gravitates toward technology when he uses his gifts while his wife, Jesi, is effective with children.

Two mistakes are common. One is to give more value to the more visible gifts. Every gift is important. The up front gifts are dependent on other behind-the-scene roles. The second mistake is to think that the roles that turn into paid professions are the most desirable ones. It is an honor to serve, paid or unpaid, and if we don't each use our gifts, there is a gap.

embrace humility

Six months before Dr. Martin Luther King, Jr. was assassinated, he spoke to a group of students at Barratt Junior High School in Philadelphia on October 26, 1967. This is what he had to say about serving with humility.

> "If you are called to be a sweeper, sweep the streets even as Michelangelo painted, or Beethoven composed music, or Shakespeare wrote poetry. Sweep streets so well that the hosts of heaven and earth will have to pause and say, 'Here lived a great street sweeper who did his job well.'"

how to get started

So how do I discover my gifts? Don't expect it to be difficult. God isn't out to play hide and seek with you. He designed your gifting to fit you like a hand fits in a glove. Look first toward the places to which your attention is naturally interested. Imagine that you have a magnet in your heart that will draw you to your gift or it to you.

more examples

John worked for the NSA translating the transmissions of Russian pilots. When he came to know Christ he naturally gravitated toward using language as his resource. He became a teacher and a pastor. Gary has a gift in making money in business. He also has the motivation for others to find what he's found. And because he recognizes God is the Provider behind every earthly resource he also has the gift of giving. Diane is a counselor who also has a gift of healing. Her discernment is off the charts. If you counsel with her, you get the best of her counseling training and a gifting that is greater than her best human efforts.

Listen for what others confirm in you. This protects you from your own subjectivity. When you hear from one and then another and another that you have a particular gift, try it out. If you don't receive encouragement, temper your enthusiasm some for that gift until you and others see some fruit. But don't be afraid to experiment. You don't always find the groove the first time.

There is a natural maturation process for each gift. Some gifts will be latent in your life during one chapter but full blown in another. Trust God's timing. Give Him a chance to do for you what you can't do for yourself. If you only do what you know you can do on your own in life, you will miss God's best.

find your sweet spot

Keep looking until you find your sweet spot. That is the place where your gifts, your passion, and your life experience come together. When you serve out of your sweet spot you will burn on instead of burning out.

You will be effective, you will enjoy it, and so will those who benefit from your ministry.

be an apprentice

Another good practice is to determine that you will apprentice under someone who is exercising the gift in the role to which you aspire. Serve as an apprentice. The term *apprentice* comes from the Middle-ages. In that day, a master craftsman would train his helper to do what he did. Gradually, the master allowed the apprentice to do more and more until the quality and craftsmanship was up to par.

the phases of ease

Dave Ferguson, the Pastor of Community Christian Church in Naperville, IL lists five stages of transition between the leader and the apprentice. First, *I do it and you watch* (then we debrief). Second, *I do it and you help* (we talk). Third, *you do it and I help* (we talk). And finally, *You do it and I watch* (we talk). Once that is complete, they both start over again with a new apprentice.[5] Even though the gift comes from God, it is important that you steward the gift and learn to use it effectively. The gift is God's gift to you. What you do with it is your gift to God.

inside the church

Some gifts fit more naturally inside the body of Christ and are used to equip and prepare the spiritual formation side of the church to be all it can be. Here are a few common examples. A gift of teaching is a huge help inside an age level ministry like children's, students', or adults'. The gift of prophecy is more *forth telling* than it is *fore telling,*and as such, it is a gift common to Pastors and leaders. Every ministry needs people with the gifts of service, discernment, and mercy. One way to think about it is that every gift can be used to serve the body of Christ that is the church, and the body needs everyone involved in ministry.

in the community

It is also true that every gift can be used outside the church. Remember, the word church doesn't mean a building, so when a gift is used outside, it means it is used with those who are exploring faith. Imagine the value of the gift of leadership in the marketplace? In the Old Testament, the first section of the Bible, there was a gift of craftsmanship. It is needed today more than ever. It could be the gift God is giving you to do your job. Don't be surprised if it is used more outside the church body than inside.

Where one might use the gifts is not always obvious. The examples above are simply for the purpose of illustration. In life, the gifts are present for every area of life both inside the world of the church and outside it. There is no need for separation between what is inside and outside the church—it is all life. Everywhere you go you are the church in action.

Invest yourself generously in others. People are the most important thing to God and serving is a privilege. Tell yourself often, *I get to do this!* When you use your gift you join the mission of Jesus to redeem and restore the children of God. You will sense the Spirit of God working through you. There is nothing like being used of God. You were made for this!

brandon michael

I wish you knew Brandon Michael. When I first met him more than three years ago now, he was fresh out of jail and a recovering drug addict. Brandon and I began a mentoring relationship shortly afterward. Brandon invited Jesus to live through him. In the beginning he attended AA meetings and after Jesus brought healing to him he became a leader at AA. Over time he found more purpose and power in directing his efforts to leading Christian based recover groups. He's gone back to school earning his Associates degree and now he is working on his BA in Christian Counseling. He recently got his driver's license back. He's reading his Bible, learning to pray, and inviting his friends to the Sunday gathering. But he also has a heart for the down and out. He takes meals to the homeless. He works tirelessly to serve others caught in the same lifestyle that once held him captive. He often volunteers at the jail mentoring those who are incarcerated.

Brandon feels called to tell others his story and share what God's done for him. Once Brandon came into my office and I asked him how it was going. He said, *I led three people to Christ this* month. Brandon feels like he's found what God wants him to do. He believes he is called to ministry. He feels called to become an ordained pastor. He's using his gifts. He's becoming like Jesus. He's living the *SENT* life! And you can, too. For additional support in discovering your spiritual gifts check out this Web Site: www.chazown.com

a prayer for gift discovery

Holy Spirit, I give you my full cooperation. Make me aware of the gifts and calling You have for my life. Show me how You want me to use what You've given me. Lead me to others. Help me find those who will help me grow. And help me find those who need what You've given me, so they can grow. In Jesus name I pray, Amen

who me? chapter 10
questions for thought or discussion

1. Do you know any other turn-around stories like Kelly's? Is your life one of those? Will you share your story?

2. Have you ever had someone tell you that they believe you have a gift? What was it? Do you agree?

3. Your Sweet Spot is defined as the place where your gifts, passion, and life experience meet. When you serve out of your Sweet Spot, you serve effectively. Describe your Sweet Spot.

4. What is one place where you enjoy serving inside the church?

5. What is a place you enjoy serving in the community?

6. What next step will you take to allow God to use the gifts He's given you?

footnotes

1. Luke 4:18-19 NIV
2. Romans 12:4-8 NIV
3. 1 Corinthians 12:4-11 NIV
4. From the estate of Dr. Martin Luther King, Jr.
5. Exponential by Dave and Jon Ferguson. Zondervan 2010.

live out

blind eyes open

"You can have it all if you are
willing to give it all away."

—Zig Ziglar

Who knew that this day would change every day afterwards?
Imagine what it would be like to be blind from birth living in the
time when Jesus lived. You wouldn't know color; only blackness.
You wouldn't know what it feels like to see a smile of approval.
You wouldn't know the face of your mother. You would fall often
and run into things. *Get out of the way,* would be normal to hear.
Left out would be the common feeling. Shame would be your
constant companion.

Surely you did something wrong to bring this on yourself. No
wait, it must have been your parents because the daylight of birth
didn't look any different than the darkness of the womb. Imagine
the mind games spent trying to figure out how it was that you
were left out when it came to something as important as sight.

This is a small piece now of how it must have felt for the blind man in John 9 when Jesus and His disciples passed by. The disciples didn't see the blind man as a person with hopes, dreams, desires, and God given potential. They saw him as an object lesson for a spiritual discussion about sin, *Rabbi, who sinned, this man or his parents, that he was born blind?*[1]

Jesus saw the blind man as a person created in the image of God with limitless potential—the same way He sees you. His limitations didn't define him in the eyes of God. *"Neither this man nor his parents sinned,"* said Jesus, *"but this happened so that the works of God might be displayed in him. As long as it is day, we must do the works of him who sent me."*[2]

Jesus lived *SENT*. He never forgot why He was here. He saw everything and everyone from this perspective. He lived out the love of God the Father every day. He came to bring light to a world walking in darkness. He was on mission, and He wasn't distracted from His purpose. He didn't treat this world as if it was all there is to life. He was here to cause heaven to kiss earth. And that was about to happen for the blind man.

After saying this, he spit on the ground, made some mud with the saliva, and put it on the man's eyes.[3] Imagine with me that you are the man born blind. You are sitting beside the road begging just like you do every day. You continually endure the scorn of others. It's hot. It's dusty. More people throw insults than throw money. Your back is tired. You are sunburned. You are thirsty. But no one cares unless you happen to get in the way. The reality is you are a burden. You know it, and so does everyone else. Then, out of the daze of these thoughts you hear a discussion going on around you. You don't recognize these voices, and that is normally one thing you do well.

Suddenly, you sense that someone is standing over you, and others are gathered around. Your heart beats faster. You've been beaten before by bullies and made fun of by groups of teens. Is that what is about to happen? Is there time to run? But which way would you go?

Somehow this feels different. It feels safe, or does it? The primary speaker's voice sounds warm and comforting. Do I know that voice? It sounds familiar. Was that person now speaking to him directly? Now, it sounds like someone is squishing mud nearby. Is someone going to hand him mud and tell him it's something to eat—that's not new.

Then before the blind man can guess what is happening, the mud is being packed into his dry eye sockets. The touch is gentle. How would one describe it? It felt like a loving caress, but he didn't have a context for a feeling like that.

Now, the one who put the mud on his eyes was speaking to him. *"Go,"* he told him, *"wash in the Pool of Siloam"* (this word means "Sent"). So the man went.[4]

The thought crossed his mind why should he trust this man? Someone said His name was Jesus. That name meant *"savior"* which was encouraging. Come to think of it, he could recall that name being thrown around in the snippets of conversation he caught as people walked passed him.

But he'd think about that later. No time to waste now. How would he find his way to the pool of Siloam? He'd gone there many times before, but he suddenly felt disoriented. Wait a minute, what if Jesus was making fun of him asking him to walk to the pool with mud on his face? He was exposed. If he cried out for help, he would draw more attention to his blindness. If he didn't cry out, he might run into someone he didn't see. This all seemed too familiar like someone was making sport of him again. It was like piling humiliation on top of shame.

But there was something different about this man Jesus. He felt a stirring in his withered soul. If there was anything he'd learned to trust it was his discernment, and now he began to feel something new. What was it? Hope? He didn't have a word for it, but he felt hopeful!

He picked up his pace. He felt compelled to get to the water. He began to exercise what little faith he had. Things were changing inside and out. This was new. It was scary and exciting at the same time. His head felt like it would explode!

He could tell people saw him coming. He knew intuitively he was causing a scene. He didn't care. What if this man was a prophet? What if God hadn't forgotten him after all? What if there was a miracle for him? He had to know!

He called for people to get out of his way, and they did. The man who was left out now became the center of attention. He was on a mission to get to the pool named *Sent*. His life was about to change forever.

He splashed water on his face and began to dig the mud away from his eye sockets. What was that? It dazed him at first. He screamed with terror or excitement; he didn't know which. It was light! And there was color! The sky was blue! He never imagined it could be so beautiful!

A crowd gathered. Amazingly, those familiar voices had faces! And people were all different sizes and shapes! The ground was a different color than the sky. He wiped more of the mud from his eyes. It helped that tears were streaming down his cheeks. Others were crying for joy, too. There was shouting, and laughing, and even shrieks of surprise! Others went to the pool jumping in hoping to get healed. But he knew it wasn't the pool that had given him sight—it was Jesus.

A decision to act in faith changed the blind man's life forever. What a great example of Jesus fulfilling His mission. The One who was living out the love of the Trinity sent the blind man to the pool named *Sent* so he too could see and live *SENT*.

The rest of the story is in John 9, and it might be shocking to learn that not everyone was happy that the blind man could now see. He immediately shared his story with great excitement, *Once I was blind but now I see*.[5] That drew him into conflict with those who didn't believe in Jesus.

tell your story

We are never the same once we experience what it means to live out the love of Jesus. When Jesus works in your life, you too will have a story to tell. The world needs to hear your story. Others will be curious, even if they don't immediately acknowledge the truth of it.

The Pharisees in the previous story debated with the man who was healed about what it all meant. They didn't share his point of view, but they couldn't deny a great miracle took place. Jesus wants to give you sight just like He did for the blind man. He wants to open your eyes to a whole new way of living. It is the lifestyle of living *SENT*.

The man wasn't born blind because someone sinned. God allowed him to be born blind because from the beginning there was a plan to use the miracle as a way to give glory to Jesus. No doubt others placed their faith in Jesus that day because the blind man exercised faith to believe Jesus and go wash in the well. Even those who missed seeing the miracle heard the amazing story.

This all fit God's plan. It was good for the blind man and good for everyone in the crowd that day. It is even good for you today as you read.

there's more for you

You were born like you were to give glory to God. Jesus doesn't make mistakes. You aren't an accident. He didn't forget you. It isn't like things have happened to you that He didn't foresee. He may not have prevented the heartache you've experienced, but neither is He finished with you yet. There is more to come to your story.

He wants to transform your weakness into strength. Is it possible that the very thing that bugs you most about yourself is what He most wants to use to teach you to trust Him? Will you give it to Him now? He has something better for you. He wants you to trade your right to be angry for His obedient acceptance of the Father's will. Will you do it?

exercise faith

Trust and faith are required on your part. These may be new exercises for you like they were for the formerly blind man. You won't always see why or how in the beginning. But as you go further down the path of obedience your miracle will start to unfold. The change will be dramatic when you start living out the love of Jesus and others will notice. Not only will it be healing for you, but it will bring joy to the heart of God. Let His love inside, and then let it live through you.

Isn't it time that you discovered your purpose and started fitting into His plan for your life? You can say to God right now, *I want to see,* and revelation will come. It often happens when we are least expecting. It usually comes to us in ways we wouldn't imagine. But it will come for you. And you will have a story to tell.

valera bachman

I have a beautiful friend named Valera. She's with Jesus now, but I'll treasure her memory forever. She was born with a birth defect that never allowed her to grow taller than four feet one inch. Her spine was so deformed that she walked in a stooped forward manner. Her lungs were under-developed, so she was often winded. Breathing was laborious for Valera, so when she spoke she usually sounded winded.

Valera knew from a very early age that she was physically deformed. She was self-conscious, in her early years, as you might expect. But early in her life she asked God to show her why He made her the way He did. She wanted to know what He had for her to do. God loves it when you ask Him that question. He came through for her.

Valera decided that God created her to be a grade school teacher. *After all,* she reasoned, *I'm their height.* They weren't afraid of her. In fact, she believed she had an unfair advantage over the other teachers because she was closer to the children physically. Every one of her students also had something for which they were also self-conscious. Her size and shape leveled the playing field for the student and teacher. They loved her.

Valera loved Jesus, and if you were around her at all you couldn't miss that. She was joyful even though she had a lot to overcome physically. I had a front row seat to her life right up until the last day, and I never heard her complain. She loved to tease and play practical jokes. She didn't see any reason why she should sit and stew over her condition. It was only temporary. She had eternity to enjoy in heaven where she would get a new body. Why should she complain now with the good that was coming?

Valera was a prayer warrior. She could storm the gates of heaven or hell with her prayers. She prayed for the children in her classes by name daily during the school year. She taught for over twenty-five years in the public school system and for over forty years in the church Sunday school classes. We will never know on earth the full effect of her life, but I'm sure it was HUGE! The only thing I couldn't understand about Valera was her love for cats. On that, we agreed to disagree!

In Valera's case, her miracle wasn't a healing that alleviated her deformity. Anyone who knew her could tell you what the miracle was. She lived with such a sense of peace and purpose that *only God* could be her Source. Many of us have much more to work with physically, and we are much poorer spiritually. The question isn't, *Why do you have what you have,* but, *what are you going to do with what you have.* Valera used her life for the glory of God! She lived out the love of Jesus in a lifestyle that was compelling.

your turn

Live out the love of Jesus. Tell your story. Live on mission every day. Don't let the past be an anchor. Forgive God. Forgive others. Forgive yourself. Live today like there is no tomorrow. Invite others into the story of God as it unfolds in your life. He is always at work bringing heaven to earth.

Ask for new eyes to see where He is at work. Instead of pouting about why He won't bless what you are doing, ask for new eyes to see what He is blessing. Join Him there. You could be living in the middle of a miracle and only see the mud if you don't follow Jesus' directions!

miracles

Don't let the talk of miracles confuse. They aren't miracles to Jesus; they are par for the course. They are normal for Him. We call them miracles because we aren't expecting them. The limitations of earth are the norm for us. Our imagination is often stunted. When the time comes to exercise faith it seems like an impossible stretch.

But where Jesus came from there is no sickness, no pain, no sin, and no death. God designed life to be lived this way on earth in the beginning before sin. This is what heaven is like now. Earth, in its' present fallen state, is the anomaly. No wonder Jesus taught His disciples to pray, *may your kingdom come. Your will be done, on earth as it is in heaven.*[6] If we took out the words, *Your will be done,* since they essentially mean the same thing as *Your kingdom come,* Jesus prayer says, *Your kingdom come on earth.* He wants what is up there to come down here.

He wants us live our lives in such a way that earth becomes more and more like heaven. And just in case you doubt that, read the story of His life and you can't miss one of his favorite themes, *the kingdom of heaven is near.*[7] Heaven is here through His ministry. You just can't see it without the eyes of faith.

dual realities

We live in a world where there are two simultaneous realities. One is eternal and limitless. We just can't physically see it. And one is human, limited, and time bound. We can see it. The second is the one where we presently exist. Faith exercised toward the will of God can bring an intersection of the two. Jesus opened the door to heaven so heaven could come to earth. He taught His followers to do the same. We aren't in control of how or when this happens, but we know the One who is. We should live our lives to continue the mission of Jesus to bring heaven to earth.

What does it look like? It looks like people discovering the Good News of Jesus. The greatest miracle ever is when a human heart truly comes to understand that God loves us. Jesus died on the cross to pay for our sin, and He offers not only forgiveness but His Spirit to live inside of us. That is the greatest miracle! Every other miracle is temporary in this life. This one is eternal. This is the greatest news the world has ever heard. It is not surprising that the Greek word used to describe this message is, *kerigma*, which is translated into English as *Good news* or *the gospel*.

share His story

As His modern day disciples, we are not only to share our story but to share His story. It is powerful. It can transform a life. It can melt a heart of stone. It can redeem a person headed for hell. It can restore a family. It can turn the heart of a father to his children and the hearts of children to their parents. Once you experience this transformation personally, you can open the door to heaven for others when you tell the gospel. It is Good news!

When you combine your story with His story, the kingdom of heaven is near and miracles happen. Give God a chance to do what He does best. We aren't responsible for the result, but often we hold the key to the kingdom of heaven. Use it for the good of others!

keven shields

I'd been praying for my neighbor, Keven, for months. He had attended Indian Creek Community Church from time to time. He was curious, but he hung out mainly on the fringes. His son, Kerby, attended Little Treasures, a learning center which is a ministry of the church.

Keven and his wife, Robyn, lived in our neighborhood. There were times he would come down to my driveway and shoot baskets with my sons Jeremy and Luke. Other times, they would play in his driveway. At times, he or Robyn asked of my sons to watch Kerby. Over time our families grew close.

One night, Keven invited me to his house to watch the Kansas University basketball game. It was an exciting game, and we were both nervous about the outcome. I admit it; I'm a big fan of KU basketball. But that night there was something even more important to me, and that was my friend's eternal destination.

At halftime, Keven changed the subject from basketball to spiritual things. He asked me a question that had been bothering him for some time about heaven and hell. It was natural to ask him where he thought he was heading at the end of his life. He said he did not know his eternal destination. I asked him if he wanted to know what the Bible said about that. He was clearly interested.

God and man, created for relationship

I shared with him a simple diagram called the bridge. God created humankind and loves us with the desire to be in relationship forever. However, God loves us so much that He also gave us free will. He won't force His love on us or preprogram us. He knows we have to choose Him for love to be real and reciprocal.

I started from the beginning with Keven. God created the earth and the people on the earth to have loving relationships.

The first two inhabitants of earth, Adam and Eve, chose selfishly. They ignored instruction from God and failed the first temptation. God's clear warning to them was that if they ate from the fruit of the tree in the center of the garden, the one that contained the knowledge of good and evil, they would die. They disobeyed because they wanted to *be like God*.[8]

Their choice set off a chain reaction of sin. The Bible calls going our own way *sin*. Their sin separated them from a Holy God. That was the spiritual death for which they were warned. Because they sinned, they opened the door to sin for everyone born after them. Every one of their descendants was born with a predisposition (literally a *bent*) to sin.

Sin enters the pic and there is a chasm between God and man

The consequence of the choice was that their sin separated them from a holy God. There was now a chasm between them wider than they could cross. The result was spiritual death.

At this point, God was grieved because He loved humankind and desired relationship. And men and women were grieved because sin never delivered what it promised. It led to dissatisfaction in life and ultimately to death and separation from God.

However, God had planned a daring rescue from the beginning of time. God sent His only born Son Jesus into the world; born of a virgin. This way, Jesus wouldn't carry the sin seed. It was transmitted from generation to generation through the line of Adam—the male gender.

The mission of Jesus was to live without sin, even though He would be tempted in every way like we are to sin. His human flesh would desire it, but if He didn't give in to sin when He died on the cross, He could die for the sin of humankind.

He did it! He paid the ultimate sacrifice! He died for the sin of the world on a cross. His death was substitution for the original sin and every one after. Since He was sinless and sin came into the world through one man, Adam, one man, Christ, could satisfy the payment of sin forever. When Christ died, the curse of sin was broken, and a way was made back to right standing with God.

There is a cross across the chasm and Death is crossed out

The cross formed a bridge across the chasm that separated God and man. Anyone who places trust in what Christ did for us on the cross for their salvation can receive forgiveness and grace from God. The key is to admit you have gone your own way. You too have sinned. Invite Christ to forgive you and lead your life.

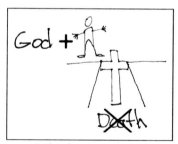

God and man are reunited

When we admit we have sinned, believe in His sacrifice, and ask for His forgiveness, we receive His grace. We cross over from death to life. We are reunited with God in relationship. We become a child of God. His Holy Spirit cleanses us and lives in us. When you make this choice, your name is written in heaven's book of life. And you become a new creation in Jesus Christ. Not only is forgiveness the ticket to heaven, but it is the way we find true life here on earth.

Keven had never heard that explanation before. I asked him if he wanted to pray to receive the free gift of God's grace. He said he did. I asked him if he would pray if I gave him some prompting. He said that he wasn't much for praying, but he would give it a try. He prayed a very simple but sincere prayer, and that day heaven touched earth.

That was years ago. Now, Keven is continually grateful he heard the Good News, and that I held the door open for him to find his way back to God. Oh, by the way, we finished praying before the start of the second half! It wasn't just the KU Jayhawks who won on that day!

share your story

If you've chosen to follow Jesus, be ready to tell your story and tell His story. Jesus calls us to follow Him and become a modern day disciple. Disciples open the door for others to follow and become disciples. It was never His plan for you to sit and soak in His grace. You are called to share it.

You are gifted to participate with Jesus in sharing life. Your gifts and life experience make it possible. You may not be the one leading everyone across the bridge but it is your life's purpose to complete the mission of Jesus by the way you live your life.

The Apostle Paul said it like this, *We are therefore Christ's ambassadors, as though God were making his appeal through us.*[9]

An ambassador lives in a foreign country but is there to carry out the business of their mother country. We live here on earth for a season but don't live to find your heaven on earth. Live to make earth more like heaven. Jesus wouldn't have called us to do it if it were not possible.

In the next chapter, we talk about how to bring heaven to earth in your neighborhood.

a prayer for Insight

Jesus, please give me Your words and the confidence that You want to use me to open the door to heaven for others. Remind me that I am to live out Your love 24/7. Thank You for the story you are creating in me. I once was blind, but now I see. Thank you for Your story that makes my story possible. Give me opportunities to share the Good News, and I will leave the results to You. Amen

blind eyes opened, chapter 11
questions for thought or discussion

1. What was miraculous about the blind beggar's story?

2. What about your own story? Have you experienced life transformation in an encounter with Jesus? How did it begin?

3. What are the dual realities; the two worlds that exist around us?

4. If you had an opportunity to share your story and His story with a friend, could you?

5. Is there someone close to you who needs to hear the Good News?

footnotes

1. John 9:2 NIV
2. John 9:3, 4 NIV
3. John 9:6 NIV
4. John 9:7 NIV
5. John 9:25 NIV
6. Matthew 6:10 NKJV
7. Matthew 10:7 NLT
8. Genesis 3:5 NIV
9. 2 Corinthians 5:20 NIV

world changer

"Never doubt that a small group of thoughtful, concerned citizens can change the world. Indeed it is the only thing that ever has."

—Margaret Mead

It started with a guitar and ultimately impacted South Africa. Tim Stout, a good friend of mine who plays the guitar, patterned his style after Paul Simon of Simon and Garfunkel fame. Tim played Simon's tunes over and over to learn the chord progressions, rhythms, and lyrics. The music wasn't the only thing that grew on him. Tim identified with soul of the musician and over time adopted a common point of view.

Tim joined protests against the Viet Nam war registering as a conscious objector. He grew his hair long. On the outside, he looked like a son of that generation. Tim and two friends formed a band that performed the music of Peter, Paul, and Mary. On the inside something was happening that would shape the rest of his life. Tim began to think beyond himself.

A common theme in the late 60's was the awareness that the world is full of injustice. A discontent deep inside of Tim with the status quo was planted decades ago that grows stronger with the passing of time.

Tim now works at Hallmark, plays the guitar for church, and for fun. Truth be told, he's still pretty serious about the guitar. He's expanded his activism considerably as he has added new interests and skill sets. Artist, photographer, and software designer describe parts of his vocation. Tim donated his time and talent to do the cover of this book and the diagrams inside. He is also a devoted family man who is a husband, father, and grandfather. His avocation is to use his talents for God and in so doing become a world changer.

Tim is a Global Champion for South Africa at Indian Creek Community Church. The holy discontent inside Tim strains to make a difference in the fight against AIDS. Multiple trips as a team leader to Kwa-dick, South Africa, gave him a firsthand understanding of the plight of a nation grappling with a national epidemic.

An idea gripped Tim's mind. What if he combined his gifts, natural talents, life experience, and marketplace skill set into the creation of a documentary? *Call Her Momma* was the award winning result. From the time he was young, Tim enjoyed telling the back story. Now, he put that passion to use in describing how one *mamma* could impact a whole city. In the process, he realized in a fresh way the impact he could have on the world around him.

Tim tells it this way, *God brought photography and South African orphans together for me. I think sometimes we ask for new abilities, new ways to "be the person God wants us to be" when all along He just wants to send us and use the abilities He already gave us. Through Him, I found a way to use my creativity to impact change.*

You too can be a world changer. Let Jesus change you first, but don't stop there. Too many of us do. Unfortunately, many of us want to follow Christ because He does so much to help us—and it is true that He does change our lives for the better. But part of following is becoming like Him. When we do, we will have a heart for helping those around us find Him, too.

It goes even further and deeper. Jesus doesn't just want to help people spiritually; though it is the most important part because it affects our relationship with God and ultimately our eternal destination. Jesus came to accomplish more. He wants to restore what was lost in the Garden of Eden. He not only wants us to be able to walk with God as Adam and Eve did,[1] but He wants earth to be more like the garden.

We are blessed to be a blessing. We are gifted to pass on God's provision to others. Don't be the end of the pipeline. Let God use you to continue His mission. This is what it means to follow Christ.

I don't like to use the word *Christian* because it means too many different things to people. It could be used to describe a nation, such as *America is a Christian nation,* when in truth, our morals or lack thereof would tell a different story. Or sometimes, it represents a person who thinks that because their name is a on a church role somewhere they are in a right relationship with God. Their goal is to meet the minimum requirements. Christ died to save us, but He lives to lead us to more than just holding on until we reach our final destination of heaven.

As a Christ follower, a Christian, our primary purpose is not just to study the Bible, huddle in a small group, and think, *Us four and no more.* We are called to follow Christ and make a difference in the world as He did.

A small band of Christ followers changed the history of the world. Jesus invested His life in them, and they invested in others, and the result is that the passion of Christ reached all the way to Tim and me and you. Don't be the end of the chain; be a door opener for others.

God said through the prophet Isaiah, *This is the kind of fasting I want: Free those who are wrongly imprisoned; lighten the burden of those who work for you. Let the oppressed go free, and remove the chains that bind people. Share your food with the hungry, and give shelter to the homeless. Give clothes to those who need them, and do not hide from relatives who need your help.*[2]

be a change agent in your world

You can do this in your corner of the world or around the world. Here's the truth about you and me. We were made for more than simply serving ourselves. You have a higher purpose or calling. Jesus wants you to join him in bringing heaven to earth. You won't have to do it alone, but there is something so unique and special with your name on it that if you don't do it, it won't get done. Jesus said, *As the Father has sent me, so I am sending you.*[3]

what does it look like?

What did it look like for Jesus to be sent? Jesus was just as comfortable confronting injustice and oppressive systems (and people) as he was healing the blind man. He taught the crowds, drove out demons, and also made time to drop in on the wedding of a friend. While attending the wedding there, He turned water into wine to save the celebration. He was working for the good of the wedding party.⁴ That is illustrative of His nature. He is always working redemptively for the good of humankind. He brings heaven to earth, and He calls you to follow Him and do what He did. And you can do it when you follow His leading.

how?

Give yourself to the simple process that follows. The Holy Spirit will lead you, and you will find a way. My friend, Tom Bassford, put these terms together: *expose, engage, and entangle.* Tim Stout naturally progressed through these phases without knowing anyone outlined the process. We can use Tim's story to discover how to create a progression for ourselves or others. If you are going to live out the love of Jesus as a lifestyle, you will likely travel the same road simply with different scenery.

expose

The beginning can be so simple it is sometimes indiscernible. You may not have a plan or even know something is going to steal your heart. In Tim's case, the first time he went to South Africa he thought he was simply providing video support for a mission trip. What happened was much more. He was exposed to the beauty, to the poverty, to the potential, and to the problems in South Africa.

You can't go to South Africa? There are opportunities around the world and around the corner. The nursery at Indian Creek Community Church's Olathe campus is often staffed by two manly men, John Bennie and Dan Ettinger. More than once, a mother entered to leave her newborn and was initially skeptical of two men offering to care for her precious little one. John and Dan have lots of experience reassuring moms that they are good at what they do. They feel called to love these newborns so their parents can hear the most important story ever told: the story of Jesus. They've served in the nursery now for over a decade. They never planned it out in advance. They simply filled a need. Caring for babies grew on them, and they found a ministry in the process.

intentionality

Other times, it can be helpful to be very intentional about an exposure opportunity. Several times in the life of the church I pastor, The Indian Creek Community Church, we've done a project called *The Church Has Left the Building*. On a selected Sunday, we have gathered briefly and then dispersed across the city to serve. The hope was never to perform a single effort and then break our arms patting ourselves on the back. We weren't looking simply for a way to salve the fact that we have more resources than the majority of the world. We wanted to meet real needs and open the door for future partnership.

We hoped to expose Creekers to community needs. The hope was that they might serve there regularly to build relationships and eventually become engaged. We had hoped that exposure to the needs and lending a hand like a Good Samaritan would become a lifestyle.

what does the world see?

All too often the only time the neighborhood sees the church gathered is when they see the cars surround a building on a Sunday. While gathering and being equipped has their place, when the people of God live out the love of Jesus they become His hands and feet to the community. Jesus said, *Whatever you did for the least of these brothers of mine, you did for me.*[5] These generous acts of service not only meet legitimate needs but are essential in order for those serving to sense God working through them. Their demonstration of God's love lived out through their lives is a breath of fresh air to a skeptical world.

Exposing people to needs is a way to get started, but it is even better when it becomes an on-ramp to a more permanent partnership. It can actually do more harm than good if the other steps don't follow. Without building relationships, it can be an act of charity that leaves the receiver feeling disempowered, unworthy, or embarrassed. Helping hurts if it enables a cycle of poverty or unhealthiness to continue unchallenged. If you asked our inner-city friends they could tell you sad stories of how suburban churches did *drive by acts of charity* that cost them more in the long run than it helped them.

Make the goal is clear from the beginning. Put a plan in place to start with relationships. Determine to empower the stakeholders or indigenous people. Give them the ownership and decision-making authority. Strive for long term partnerships. Commit to address the systemic nature of the problem in order to create lasting transformation.

engage

Participation in multiple exposures to service will help you discover one or more that results in a longer term investment. Look for one that feels like a fit. This is a place to engage. Return to serve there several times to experience it during the various seasons of the year. Learn the names and faces of those you serve and those with whom you serve. It is not uncommon to take home information or research it on the Web. You'll probably tell some friends and invite them to go with you the next time. What began as someone else's project has now become personal. Before you realize it you may find yourself praying for the needs and even giving financially. You are engaged.

larry and kathy endecott

Larry and Kathy didn't know what to expect the first time that they volunteered. They attended a *First Serve* opportunity at Indian Creek and Community Church that took them to the inner-city of Kansas City, Kansas. They served at The Urban Scholastic Center, a ministry led by Chuck Allen and his staff. They were impressed.

USC was under-resourced and the community needed more than what they could give in a day, or a lifetime for that matter. Larry and Kathy decided to return weekly. They found opportunities to serve that fit their gift mix. Before long, they became so committed that they woke up thinking about ways to change that corner of the world.

entangled

No doubt there will be a place where, over time, the needs will capture you at a heart level. You may be inspired to start a ministry that doesn't exist to meet an unmet need. Serving gives you the chance to discover your sweet spot. When you do you'll find living out the love of Jesus isn't a burden but a joy.

While on your day job, you'll find yourself problem-solving for your new passion. At night, you'll lie on your bed thinking of ways to improve. You'll pray for the people there by name. You'll not only give regularly, but you'll find yourself picking up supplies when you run to the hardware or grocery. It has become a part of your life. This is good! You are entangled.

Every follower of Jesus is called to be a missionary (one who lives *SENT*) and most of us don't get paid for what we do! The mission field starts at the doorstep of your home. You can go halfway around the world, but you don't have to in order to be a world changer.

terry geenens and countryside

Terry Geenens began serving at Countryside Grade School because Tom Bassford, the Live Out Director at Indian Creek Community Church, asked the right question of Stacy Shipley, the principal, of the local grade school.

How can we serve you? It seemed a simple way to begin.

That question launched a six year ministry that is still growing. Stacy, the principal, knew in her heart that without the help of parents, the community, and the church, the large number of unmet needs would impair the learning environment she hoped to create. She was ecstatic that Terry visited her school.

A volunteer at Indian Creek Community Church, Cheryl Johnson, had already built trust with the Countryside staff and students. She scouted out numerous opportunities where individuals or the church could serve. She dropped hints right and left that the church should be involved in the school. When Terry showed up, Cheryl and Stacy knew it was only a matter of time before she would fall in love with the kids. They were right.

Terry worked tirelessly to involve others in kidzAlive! and in the larger church body. New ideas emerged. Backpacks were needed to start the school year. Some students couldn't afford their school picture or the Countryside T-shirt and felt left out. *We could help*, were the words that came out of Terry's mouth.

These children also needed meals during the holidays when school wasn't in session. Many of the children had single parents and one-third of the school population lived at or below the poverty level. Thirty some children were homeless. They needed mentors, lunch friends, and extra sets of hands for field trips. A year into the partnership Stacy asked Terry if they could do a Summer Camp together. The church already did a VBS but we changed the name and invited the community. More and more people caught the vision and partnerships grew between the school, the church, the community, and the business world.

The latest project is a Life Enrichment Center where under-resourced children are bused to Indian Creek Community Church after school to learn, cultural arts, life skills and develop character. The Deputy Superintendent of the school district, Dr. Allison Banikowski, and the Mayor, Mike Copeland, took note. They put together a task force to campaign that every school in the Olathe School District would have a church and corporate partner.

Within the Countryside partnership, there are people at all three of the different stages. Some are just getting exposed. Many are engaged at some level. Others are entangled. Terry resigned her job at the church as the KidzAlive! director to become a volunteer at Countryside, a coordinator of Indian Creek's work at the school, and to direct the Life Enrichment Center. There she combines her educational training as a teacher with her heart that the children will have what they need to succeed in life.

find your place

There is a place for you. Start simple and small. Start with what you have. What natural abilities do you have? Your skills, gifts, talents, and resources were entrusted to you for more than simply your own benefit.

What is your holy discontent? How could you use your life experience to make a difference in your world? Could there be a way these could come together in a place of service? Where would you invest and give back? Start somewhere and follow the leading of the Holy Spirit. You will know in the appropriate time where to put down your roots. The relationships will be a fit. You will find your heart engaged when the time and place is right. You won't have to manufacture it. It won't be like you have to work up motivation to serve. You will discover God's plan. It will flow powerfully from God through you. You will someday say, *I was made for this!*

a prayer of dedication

Jesus, I dedicate myself to living out Your love. I'll do what You ask me to do. I thank You in advance for doing what only You can do. Together, we can bring heaven to earth and make earth more like heaven. Thank You for this high calling and the anointing of Your Spirit to get it done. Amen

world changer, chapter 12
questions for thought or discussion:

1. Have you been surprised by a desire to serve similar to the passion that gripped Tim Stout's heart?

2. Reread the Isaiah passage and make a list of the desires of God that target injustice.

3. What does it mean to be exposed, engaged, and entangled?

4. What are your unique gifts, experiences, and circumstances, which God can use to bring Heaven to earth through you?

5. Do you know someone who has become entangled in the needs of others?

footnotes

1. Genesis 3:8 NIV
2. Isaiah 58:6–7 NLT
3. John 20:21 NLT
4. John 2:1–11
5. Matthew 25:40 NIV

sent

say yes

"Saying yes to what God says yes to is the supreme
understanding of the Lordship of Christ in the believer's life."

—R.S. Nicholson

*You are going to be asked to go to China and India and when
you are, you are to say "Yes."* Those were the words I heard in my
head as I walked out of a conference center after speaking to a
group of pastors in Monterrey, Mexico. It was both confusing and
exciting to hear!

Where did that thought come from? From God? I didn't even
know anyone planning trips to Asia. If those thoughts came from
God there must be some adventure coming my way. It all felt
rather surreal. Was I imagining it?

Less than a minute later, I walked into a conversation with
Donna Thomas, the Founder and the President of Project Partner.
The first words she spoke to me were in the form of a question.
She said, *Will you go to China and India with me?*

Without any hesitation I answered her, *Yes!*

Shocked, she responded, *No one ever says, "Yes," the first time I ask them!*

Well, if you experienced what I had just experienced you would say "Yes" too. I replied.

I told her the back story. She was ecstatic! I was in a daze. What just happened? In the next few years, I did go to India twice and then to China multiple times. Years later, Donna asked me to lead Project Partner, an international ministry, now focused on China.

I found someone else who felt led to say, *Yes.* Kristen Levitt, my daughter, agreed to be the Director of Project Partner. I feel called to give Indian Creek Community Church my primary focus. Kristen can give Project Partner (www.projectpartner.org) the full-time energy and skill the ministry requires.

Kristen was interested in missions from sixth grade forward. While at Taylor University, she believed God was leading her to serve in a mission ministry. She just didn't know where or when. She sensed it would be in the United States. She suspected she would use her communication skills to travel, recruit, and raise funds for ministry in a foreign country. Project Partner was the perfect fit. Now my wife, Belinda, and I both serve regularly with Kristen in China and at home in Olathe where Project Partner is headquartered. Belinda also travels to India annually to lead teams of women to teach in training conferences.

Here's the point of the story, and it is not about me or my family. It is for you. Dare to say *Yes.*

I know there is an appropriate process in decision making, and I don't want to undermine that, but make your default response *Yes* instead of *No.* Unless you have a negative prompting in your spirit lead with a *Yes, Yes* once doesn't mean *yes* forever. You can decide the frequency later. You may never know what adventures with the Holy Spirit you will miss if you close the door before you ever begin.

You've heard the starter in a race say, *Ready, set, go.*But there are times when you won't be ready. You won't always have your ducks in a row. Everything won't be set, but if you don't go when the door opens, it might not open again.

Maybe there is also a place for *Not ready, set, go!* You will never know it all, have enough money, time, talent or energy, but go anyway. Is it scary just to read these words? Absolutely, if you think that God might be leading you to say *Yes*. Sometimes, you have to go forward in faith, despite the reality that your knees are knocking in fear. This is how you learn to depend on God.

There will no doubt be some *No's*. If you don't say *No* to something you won't have the margin to say *Yes* to other things. At times, God might even redirect you from a course you thought you should take. Perhaps you said *Yes*, and God wants you to wait or do something different. Embrace that as a win that you were willing. Graciously accept His correction, and let it embolden you for the next time because it is obvious He will lead you if you are on the wrong path. Don't be afraid to decide. Learn to listen to the Spirit and your spouse, if married, and be ready to say *Yes!*

it works like this

Practice this with me. Would you like to attend a prayer retreat? *Yes.* Would you participate in community group or missional community? *Yes.* Will you lead in family devotions tonight? *Yes.* Will you go on a mission trip? *Yes.* Will you support someone else who feels called to go? *Yes.* Will you help start a new church or campus? *Yes*. Decision making becomes a lot easier when we plan to say *Yes* unless otherwise prompted to say *No*.

Prayerfully and thoughtfully consider your schedule, family, financial and work constraints. Focus is a good thing. But it is way too easy to let *No* be our default. We will never know what we, by God's grace, can do if we don't allow Him to stretch us beyond our comfort zone.

Living *SENT* requires that we venture beyond the safety of our comfort zone. Don't put God in a box. He is God, and you are not. Practice trust and dependence on God by regularly allowing God to stretch you. Take time to read Hebrews 11, and you will find a Hall of Fame for those who said *Yes*. My guess is that they didn't have all the answers, but they excelled at faith.

Faith is the confidence that what we hope for will actually happen; it gives us assurance about things we cannot see...by faith Abel brought a more acceptable offering to God than Cain...by faith Noah built a large boat to save his family from the flood. He obeyed God, who warned him about things that had never happened before...by faith Abraham obeyed when God called him to leave home...and without faith it is impossible to please God.[1]

Steering a car is a lot easier when it is moving. Start saying *Yes* and God will steer you into new territory. It will stretch you and build your faith.

Do you know people who are great at doing one thing well? They only want to do what they can master. Be careful, sometimes what we call a desire for excellence is really a fear of getting outside our expertise. We don't have the luxury of only taking on only those things in which we can excel.

My experience with following God tells me God will continually test any places I'm unwilling to yield to Him. If there are places where I want to be in control, I find He regularly moves me out of my little box to help me think like He thinks.

lost!

One summer day Belinda took our only vehicle, our van, and left me at home with all three of our kids. She had her doubts, but I convinced her I could do it. I actually felt confident about it, imagine that! Our three children, Kristen, Jeremy, and Luke, were grade school age at that time of their lives.

I was doing my best when I realized that Luke, our youngest, who was about five years of age, was not around. He liked to hide from us, so I assumed this was a game. I looked in all the normal places and called for him until I was no longer amused. I went outside and noticed the gate to our fenced backyard in our suburban neighborhood stood wide open! Our Dalmatian, *Princess*, was gone, too!

Oh great, I thought, I've lost a kid and the dog. *Lord please don't let Belinda come home now!*

The minutes seemed to crawl as I searched desperately for Luke. I called his name from every corner of our yard all the while aware I had two other children to watch inside. Every minute lost meant that the chances of finding him decreased. What if he was in trouble? What if someone had kidnapped him? What if he was in pain?

I don't have words to describe the knot in my throat and the sick feeling in my stomach. I had flashbacks of when our daughter, Megan, died. I felt paralyzed and frantic at the same time. If you've been through something like that, you know what I'm talking about, and you never forget it.

It didn't matter to me at that moment that I still had two kids who were safe. One was lost! That was what mattered most!

I stood in the front yard and created a plan with a mental checklist. I would need to farm the kids out to the neighbors, call the police, and start a search.

At that moment, Luke appeared at the end of the block, hot and exhausted, dragging an unwilling dog behind him. The story was that *Princess* got out, and Luke followed her all the way to the neighborhood park. She had been headed for the nearby creek. He had caught her by the chain and brought her back. My knees went weak from relief. I wanted to shout but what came out was more like a cry. My son was alive and he was coming home!

This is a picture of the desire God has for every one of His children who are lost, and by that I mean with whom He doesn't have a relationship. If you do have a relationship with God, He doesn't love you less. He loves all of His children equally. As much as He loves you, you need to know there is more to life than just you!

It is tempting to find our way back to God, and then play defense the rest of our days. Self protection mode feels natural. Why not just hole up and hold on until heaven?

Are you aware of the passionate heart's desire of Your Father to bring all His children home?

I pray often, *Lord, break my heart with the things that break your heart. Give me Your passion for those who don't yet know you.* Would you pray that prayer with me daily?

new birth

Have you ever experienced the joy and wonder of witnessing the very moment a mother gives birth? It is messy! It is painful and suspense-filled! It is also more rewarding than words can express. If you've been in the labor and delivery room, you probably had a thought similar to what I had when Belinda gave birth to our children, *This is the reason we live!* It is exhilarating! Just think you had a part in creating a child! An eternal soul was just born, and you are the parent! It doesn't get any better than that!

We are meant to pass on life to others. It's not about us. The truth is, it never was, but it just took us a while to get it.

the prodigal

We love the story of the Prodigal Son[2] especially the part about the Father waiting for the son to return home. When the son came home the Father greeted him with arms wide open and all was restored. We read the story and picture ourselves as the son who came home. Typically, we don't identify with the son who stayed.

But often we completely miss another significant part of the story. Our clue rests in the audience that listened as Jesus related the story. Jesus told the story to the Pharisees. This group of people would have known that (in Jewish culture) the elder brother should have gone out to find the younger son and bring him back. That would have been his role. It would have been expected of the older brother. It wasn't appropriate just to stay at home and play it safe if your younger brother was lost.

The father in the story needed to stay home. If he had pursued the younger son, it might have made the son run further faster. The prodigal might not have come to his senses and made the personal choice to return. But the elder brother didn't do what he could have done. He could have gone after his wayward brother. He didn't. His life was okay. It may have even been a little easier. As long as his life was okay, he was fine with that. It wasn't his problem, or so he thought.

The older brother wasn't living a life that was *SENT*, was he? We are often too comfortable thinking about the concerns of our lives while our family, friends, neighbors, and co-workers are wandering away from the Father. Most days, we are okay with that. Are we like the older brother? If it doesn't affect me, I'm not concerned?

I'm often uncomfortable about my lifestyle, and I hope you are uncomfortable reading this chapter. It usually takes some discomfort to change. I evaluate and reevaluate my priorities and how I use my time and energy. Until the fear of staying the same outweighs the fear of change, we usually stay the same. I'm afraid if I am not vigilant in caring for my brothers, my heart will grow complacent. I want to be connected with the heart of my Father. When I am, I'm aware of those around me who need my help to find their way back to the Father.

life is not about comfort

Life here is not about our comfort, and the sooner we realize that the better. No wonder Jesus said, I must be about my Father's will.[2] Are you willing to allow Him to break your heart with the things that break His heart? What will you do about it?

promptings

Be open to the Holy Spirit's leading. Within this book are multiple stories where I've heard things which I think originated from God. They usually come into my mind as a thought. I don't hear a particular voice in my head. They are much like any other thought. I think we all have them. I'm not super spiritual, and I don't always get it right, but I am willing to listen and obey. Are you?

Sometimes I will get it wrong, but if my motives are right, and I don't play the God card where I say, God told me to tell you most mistakes are repairable. Don't be afraid to be wrong. The more you act on what you think God is saying the better you will become at hearing. And if you are faithful with what God trusts to you, He will give you more. Conversely if you ignore God and tune Him out, you hear less and less.

We don't always have the benefit of carefully contemplating every option life gives. Opportunities sometimes appear and time is of the essence. If you miss the moment, you don't always get that chance back. I encourage you to give God your undivided attention when you think you may be prompted of God. Lead with a *Yes*. When you do, you are on your way to some of the most delightful experiences, and I've had some of the most delightful and challenging experiences in life. This is the lifestyle of one who lives *SENT*.

say yes, chapter 13
questions for thought or discussion

1. Are there times where you have a thought that you believe came from God? Give an example.

2. Share a time where you led with a *Yes*. How did it turn out?

3. Discuss the merits of both statements: *Ready, set go* and *Not ready, not set but go anyway*.

4. Have you ever become separated from someone dear to you? Describe it. How did you feel? Does it help you understand how God feels?

5. With whom do you most identify in the story of the prodigal son?

6. What is it that God would have you say *Yes* to?

footnotes
1. Hebrews 11:1-8 NLT
2. Luke 15:11-32

unplanned adventure

"The only thing necessary for the triumph of evil
is for good men to do nothing."

—Edmund Burke

Look at the life of Jesus. Many of His encounters appear unplanned. They were spontaneous, and He was always up for a good conversation. One such was the story of the Good Samaritan.

A Jewish man was traveling on a trip from Jerusalem to Jericho, and he was attacked by bandits. They stripped him of his clothes, beat him up, and left him half dead beside the road.

By chance a priest came along. But when he saw the man lying there, he crossed to the other side of the road and passed him by. A Temple assistant walked over and looked at him lying there, but he also passed by on the other side.

Then a despised Samaritan came along, and when he saw the man, he felt compassion for him. Going over to him, the Samaritan soothed his wounds with olive oil and wine and bandaged them.

*Then he put the man on his own donkey and took him to an inn,
where he took care of him. [35]The next day he handed the
innkeeper two silver coins,[e] telling him, 'Take care of this man. If
his bill runs higher than this, I'll pay you the next time I'm here.'*

*Now which of these three would you say was a neighbor to
the man who was attacked by bandits?" Jesus asked.*

The man replied, "The one who showed him mercy."

Then Jesus said, "Yes, now go and do the same."[1]

I need to read this story because it challenges my life. The way
I use my time, my sensitivity toward my brother, how I treat others of a different culture, and my willingness to work on God's
timetable are just a few of the lessons to learn.

Many times, I gravitate toward the well worn ruts of my life
that protect me from the unknown. The Samaritan made good
choices. He didn't try to save himself from everything that
could have gone wrong. Ultimately, that was beyond him anyway. He made the time. He risked. He got involved. He
invested in the wounded man's healing and knew when to
move on. The Samaritan left the wounded man in the care of
someone else at his own expense until he could return to
check on him later. He didn't have to do all of that, but that
story ends very differently for the wounded man if the
Samaritan doesn't do what he can do.

for what are you saving yourself?

Not one of us is guaranteed tomorrow. If tomorrow does
come the same God who has lovingly provided for us thus far will
take care of that one, too. Planning and preparation are good
disciplines. I agree we need to *Work like there is no tomorrow
but plan like you'll live a long life.* However, don't let your plans

become your god. Be open to the Holy Spirit and open to people if you want to live *SENT*.

The Bible doesn't relate, *the rest of the story,* as Paul Harvey used to say on his nationally syndicated radio show. I wish we knew it if there was one.

I wonder if the Good Samaritan was willing to address the systemic nature of the problem. I imagine that it was well known that robbers frequented that particular stretch of the road. A person living *SENT* would not only be spontaneous to help one in need but also would want the kingdom of heaven to come to earth.

part two

Since the story is a parable anyway let's have a little fun with it and imagine a part two. If the Samaritan was living *SENT*, he might go find a person who was an engineer to look for ways to straighten the road and take out the hiding places. Maybe he would find an investor or donor who would pave it and put in lighting.

Perhaps, he needed to visit the local police and see if they could patrol the area regularly. If the police force was under-manned and over challenged, would he recruit civil servants?

The one who is living *SENT* is continually thinking about how earth could become more like heaven. You may be a part of the solution. You may be the answer to your own prayers or someone else's.

God can use you! Things here on earth change when people dare to believe God can use us. He will use anyone who is willing. Whatever your limitations, they aren't as big as His greatness. No problem you will ever face is greater than God. You and God are always a majority, and when you add in the rest of the body of Christ, you'll have what you need.

parents

Listen up parents! In the book of Psalms, there is a scripture that warms the heart of most parents, *Children born to a young man are like arrows in a warrior's hands. How joyful is the man whose quiver is full of them! He will not be put to shame when he confronts his accusers at the city gates.*[2]

I get the warm fuzzies just thinking about a quiver full of arrows with multiple colors on the end of the shaft. I just want to mount the quiver, like the pictures of my children on the mantle, and look at it often. Every now and then, I'll take it down and lovingly caress it—look at my children! How angelic they look in the picture. How special they are to me. I love them so much. I won't let anything happen to them! I'll do anything I can to keep them from harm. You get the picture, right!

But that is not the metaphor the Bible is using. The purpose of an arrow is to be sent. Arrows are for shooting. How else would the man confront the accusers at the city gate? The Psalmist wasn't glowing over his accumulation of arrows or children. He wanted to win the battle.

I love my family dearly, but the Bible tells me we are at war with one who comes to *Steal, kill and destroy.*[3] The enemy doesn't play fair, and he doesn't care about what is important to you. His one mission is to overthrow the plan of God, and he is hell bent on undermining it anyway he can. We can't sit out or opt out of this battle even if we want to. The battle will come right to you and your home. Don't try to make peace with the enemy by asking for a truce. All you'll get is lies and false assurances. It is an illusion to stay out of his way so that you can protect yourself and all that you hold dear. He is the enemy of God and anyone that loves God.

your protection

Our protection is only in Jesus who is our Savior. Jesus is undefeated. He is the One who said we would press the battle to the gates of hell itself, and we will recover those held captive.[5] The safest place to be on earth is the center of His will.

I began ministry by serving as a Youth Pastor. I worked with youth for many years, and long ago I lost count of how many mission trips I led. I can say the following with confidence. Many parents are over protective of their children. The idea that parents can ultimately protect their children from all problems in life does them more harm than good. It doesn't teach them to depend on their Creator who alone can protect and provide for them. Neither does it allow them to develop problem solving skills. They are likely to miss the unplanned adventures God has if playing it safe is the default mode in their home.

Please consider that with that behavior you may, in fact, NOT be preparing your children to succeed in life. Safety in this world is mostly just an illusion. This is a painful truth! However, it is also true that in Christ you are safe enough. It is better to put your children in places where they will learn to trust God and fight for themselves in a spiritual way than to send the signal that the most important thing in life is safety. The sooner they learn that the better.

Christianity is not about digging a foxhole and hiding hoping against hope that you can stay out of the line of fire until you arrive safely at death and say, *I did it!* Did what? Did you have perfect attendance at worship services? Did you attend Bible studies that went deeper? Did you learn the meaning of the Hebrew and Greek words? What was the purpose?

deeper equals obedience

Obedience at any cost is the goal. Nothing spurs spiritual growth like sacrifice in service. Often, I hear Christians say they want something *deeper*. Usually the context for that comment is in relationship to a message they heard while safely sitting in a church gathering. If you want a biblical definition for *deeper*, it would be obedience. Deeper is usually developed in the middle of the action. A disciple is a person in the process of becoming just like his master. Dare we settle for something less? Some who claim to believe aren't following—that isn't deeper, and it isn't obedience. God has something much better for you.

SENT

The truth is that we aren't here to live for ourselves. Dare to believe that the Father wants 100% obedience and that you can give it. Jesus did! I like what Bill Hybels says, *95% devotion is 5% short.*

Be aware of this trap. You will be tempted to play both sides of the equation. A person says he wants God's will but then isn't willing to do what God asks of him. The result is a life that is filled with unfulfilled convictions and weak faith. Lack of spiritual fulfillment is then blamed on the church because the person isn't growing. In truth, the lack of growth was caused by a lack of obedience.

Your life mission will test you beyond what you think you can bear. But humbly depend on the Spirit and be willing to do without anything. Embrace sacrifice and surrender. It brings unimaginable joy!

Learn any lesson you need to learn, and He will get you to the finish line. Your race might finish shorter than you imagined, or God may have plans for you to live into your golden years. But you can be sure about this—you won't die one day before God's perfect will for you is achieved. Your life is in His hands, and there is no better way to live than to live SENT.

a prayer of servanthood

Jesus, I give You everything. I lay it all down—my safety, my comfort, my will, and my plan for life. My life is not my own. I give up my rights to Your control. I want to know Christ whatever it takes. I want to fulfill Your will for my life. I will love You God with all my heart, soul, mind and strength and I will love my neighbor as myself. I will spend every day for the rest of my life living out the love of Jesus. I will live SENT.

unplanned adventure, chapter 14
questions for thought or discussion

1. Have you ever stopped to help someone like a Good Samaritan? Share the story.

2. Are you willing to be a part of the longer term solutions for the needs in your community, or world? In what way?

3. Are you a parent? Have you ever thought that your children were given to you to be SENT?

unplanned adventure | 165

4. What are some ways we are tempted to play it safe?

5. In light of what you read, what is one thing you will change?

6. Will you give your fears to God in prayer and ask Him to fill you with bold faith?

footnotes
1. Luke 10:30-37
2. Psalm 127:4, 5 NLT
3. John 10:10 NIV

wrong song

"It's not about you."

—Rick Warren

If you learned a Christian song in the early years of your life, there is a good chance you learned *Jesus Loves Me*. If you need a refresher on the lyrics, it goes like this. Sing out loud if you'd like.

Jesus loves me this I know
for the Bible tells me so
Little ones to him belong
They are weak but he is strong

Chorus: *Yes, Jesus loves me*
Yes, Jesus loves me
Yes, Jesus loves me
The Bible tells me so

How can you help but smile when you sing that song? I break into a grin just thinking about it. There is a reason we love that song, and it goes beyond the fact that it is true. We love it because it is about us. Jesus loves ME! I love that! There's nothing wrong with that, right?

To capture the full spirit of the song, we might as well wrap our arms around ourselves when we sing it. *Jesus loves me*. What a comfort that is! Try it. It makes you feel good. Please don't burn me for heresy. I like the song. I really do, but it can be a problem too. If I'm honest, I want everything to be about me. *Me, me, me* is the song we like to sing.

The whole idea of the title of the book, *Backwards*, is that to make everything about me feels so appropriate. Yet it is opposite of the way God wants us to think. We think it is all about me. And the truth is—it's not about me.

We naturally make ourselves the center of the story. Our first filter in life is the one that judges something good or bad, right or wrong, by how it affects me. We all do it. And it is backwards to the way that God designed life.

This truth, that Jesus loves me, is a basic building block for life. And remember, with God it IS all about you—that is why He sent Jesus die on the cross—to pay for your sin. But once you follow Him—it is no longer about you, it is about OTHERS. Jesus wants everyone to know Him. Once you join the family of God, it is the pre-occupation of this family to live your life on mission, on purpose, all the time for others to know Jesus. It's not about you. That is the plan, and it is a good thing.

Trust him to meet your needs as you serve. Trust his love as you go through your life. It will always be there for you. When you live the life that is *SENT* there is a divine return cycle that is better than any you could create on your own. You become your brother's keeper. And God becomes your keeper. To the extent that we live with this perspective life makes sense.

missed the point

History is full of examples where people got half the story right. They rightly understood that God loved them, but they missed the second half of the truth—that because He did, they were to orient themselves toward others. As a result they misunderstood what God wanted to do with them. They were confused concerning his will because they didn't get it that their motivation was backwards to his.

I call these cases, *adventures in missing the point*. It was more the norm than the exception in the scriptures. I hate to admit it but it is the dominant reaction from God's people today. Whenever we find God's blessing, we also find the temptation to think the reason we are blessed is for selfish purposes. That's a bold statement so go with me on a search through the scriptures.

exodus

The book Exodus is titled appropriately. The Hebrew people rejoiced to escape 430 years of slavery in Egypt. Of course they did! The Hebrews loved it that they were God's chosen people. The way He rescued them from the Egyptians was incredible! It was awesome to be on the winning team.

There were ten plagues that revealed the miraculous power of Yahweh, the Almighty God of Israel, which brought Egypt to its knees. By the time they left the Egyptians were so glad to see them go that they sent them out with their jewelry as a blessing. God split the Red Sea for them and they went through on dry

ground. He let the waters return and it drowned their enemies—
what a dramatic reversal to eliminate the competition!

God guided the children of Israel with a pillar of fire at night
and a cloud by day. He gave Moses the 10 Commandments, and
the Elders got to eat a meal in the presence of God. He gave
them manna to eat and brought water from a rock. They began
to think, *this is all about me*. If you strain you could hear the first
chorus of *Jesus Loves ME ME ME* from the Sinai desert.

The way God was working everything for their good it was a
baby step from there to believing God was all about making
them happy and meeting their needs. We know this because
whenever God didn't meet their needs the way they wanted,
they wanted a new God. A case in point was the very instance
that God gave the Ten Commandments.[1]

Moses was invited into the presence of God on Mount Sinai,
and the people waited in the valley below. But we all know that
selfishness is not good at waiting. When Moses didn't return in
a comfortable time frame, they made their own god in the form
of the same idol that was defeated months earlier as they left
Egypt.

on mission

This was an adventure in missing the point. While it was true that
God did love them it was also true that His work in them was a
means to an end not just an end in itself. They were blessed to be
a blessing. Ultimately, it wasn't about them. In God's plan they were
on a mission to bring light into the world so the world would know
that there is a God in heaven and that He loves every person.

They thought they had the option of telling God *Thanks, but
no thanks. I'll follow you if it is good for me and only if it is good*

for me. They thought they deserved the right to offer selective obedience. However, selective obedience is disobedience.

They forgot who they were,and why they existed. They lost their identity. They were the children of God. They lived to be an example of God's love. Their identity was wrapped in the redemptive plan of God. God the Father loved his Son, Jesus, but still the Father sent his son to the cross.

The nature of love is that it puts the beloved first. Jesus said he went to the cross for *the joy that was set before him.*[2] The cross was the pathway to forgiveness and freedom for the captives he loved— you and me. This is the DNA in every Christian put there by the Holy Spirit's presence.

self preservation

The Hebrews didn't understand their heritage. This was evident when they balked at entering the Promised Land of Canaan. If it meant war to take possession of the land it was too risky. If self preservation is your goal, you don't invade enemy territory.

Who were these people? If they were simply escaped slaves then they should avoid conflict. If they were wandering nomads, they should live in the desert. If they were spoiled brats, they should be able to sit on their heritage and wait for God to do everything for them. But if they were *the people of God sent on a mission to share His light and love until the whole world knows*—then they should be ready to fight.

identity

You will never find your identity in simply watching how things happen in the world around you. You will not find your identity by looking to others around you to see what they say. You won't even find your identity by looking in the mirror. You certainly won't find your identity by looking in your past. You will only find your identity by looking into the eyes of Your Creator. He put the image of God in you—you must get in touch with that!

He has a plan for you that is good for you, yes. But it is not about you and you alone. You can sing, *Jesus Loves Me.* It is true. It is a good place to begin, but a terrible place to stop.

The children of Israel missed the point. God wanted them to be His chosen people so they could display His glory, His truth, and His love. He did miracles for them so that they would be his instrument to reach the world. But they refused to obey Him if it wasn't in their self interest to do so. They missed the point, and they missed the Promise Land.

As a result, that first generation wandered 40 years in the desert until they died to self and literally died. Finally after the sense of entitlement was gone, God had a people He could use. God took his children right back to their place of failure. When they rightly understood their identity and their purpose in life they took possession of the Promised Land.

The truth is—everything we have is given for us to use, not only for our needs, but for redemption's plan. Our needs get met along the way as we live the life that is *SENT.* We too *are the people of God sent on a mission to bring light and love to the world until the whole world knows.*

get it straight

When they got that straight—they claimed their promised land. The same will be true for you. But for some reason there are times in the life of most Christ followers were they feel free to give God the Heisman. Go ahead, strike the pose. We hold out our hand as if to fend off the will of God when it doesn't please our selfish plan.

Here is my concern. You could go to any church and think, *The church is here for me. I need this and that delivered in my desired way and if I don't get it, I'm outta here.* You wouldn't say, *It is all about me.* But your consumer's attitude would give it away.

With this attitude we don't want a God, someone who will lead our life down a self sacrificing path, we want a genie in a bottle. We treat prayer like it is a means to an end not a relationship of dialog and surrender. We want to rub the bottle and get the result of our three wishes. We think, *It is my life. It's my choice as to how I serve and God should be happy with whatever I give him.*

You need to know this, with God it is always about worldwide redemption.

God is moving in this world in the direction of redemption, and if you don't move with Him, you get left behind. He still loves you, but He is moving. Of course, you have a choice. You can go with God, or you can stay stuck right where you are. He will keep moving, and you will be left behind. His love is unconditional. His blessings are totally conditional based on your obedience.

Memorize this statement with me: *I am sent on a mission to bring light and love to the world until the whole world knows.*

Often it is easier to see selfishness in someone else's life so let's look at another adventure in missing the point. Roll history forward to the Bible story of Jesus cleansing the temple.[3]

cleansing the temple

Jesus went to the temple to worship but what he found was so disturbing that he overturned the money changer's tables and stopped anyone from carrying merchandise through the temple courts. He was livid! The Jews had created a marketplace. He made a whip of rope and he drove the animals and the vendors out.

The common interpretation of this story is that it is upsetting to God that a store would be set up in the temple. That is overly simplistic! Read the story, and you will find the clue in Jesus' words.

He said, *My house shall be a house of prayer.*[4] Don't stop reading there. If you do, you may miss the point. The point of the story had nothing to do with selling things in church. It is not even about prayer being the priority—which is the focus of numerous sermons based on this story.

What fired up the passion of Jesus was this: they way they went about their worship prevented the mission of redemption! The Jewish worshippers might as well have cued the choir to sing *Jesus loves me this I know—and that's all I know.* They were so narrowly focused on their Jewish experience it was as if the rest of the world didn't matter.

Jesus' pointed message to them was, *My house shall be a house of prayer for ALL nations.*[5] (emphasis mine)

A little history helps here. The Jews set up the market in the only place the Gentiles could pray—in the court of the Gentiles. The temple was constructed for all, the Jews and the Gentiles. The plan of God for the temple set aside a courtyard for non-Jews to connect with God in prayer.

This was the very place the Jews set up the market to sell animals that would be used by the Jews when they offered their sacrifices. They were so certain that it was all about them that they made prayer for the Gentiles impossible. The way they did church excluded the very people Jesus would later die to reach. They missed the point of worldwide redemption.

Worship wasn't just for the Jew! They were to be light and love until the whole world knew the love of God. The Jews were *God's chosen people*, right? But they forgot the reason they were chosen. God chose a people who would be his example to display his nature and truth to the world.

light and love

I can see this happening to followers of Jesus today if we don't keep our motives straight on why we are here. We could construct our lifestyle and even our churches to fit our own purposes. We can use insider language. We can create traditions that become ritual devoid of mission. We can live our lives in a way that excludes the very redemptive purpose of the life of Jesus. We can create our own adventure in missing the point.

We would do well to memorize this mission statement: *We are the people of God sent on a mission to share His light and love until the whole world knows.*

One more story, Jesus, before he ascended into heaven, gave a very clear mandate to his disciples concerning his mission. Now it was their mission.

He said, *You will be my witnesses Jerusalem, Judea, Samaria and to the ends of the earth.*[6]

redemption

The focus was redemption. The audience was the world. Jesus also told them to wait until the Holy Spirit filled them before they tried to fulfill the mission in their own human strength.[7]

The disciples rounded up those who believed in Jesus, and they prayed together in an upper room for ten days. I'm sure they didn't know exactly what they were waiting for or what it would look like, but they knew they would know when it happened.

On the day of Pentecost, fifty days after Easter, the Holy Spirit came in such a powerful way that it was like the blowing of a mighty wind. They were under the influence of the Holy Spirit and it led them out of the prayer service into the street. They proclaimed the wonder of God with such energy they quickly drew a crowd.

The Jewish Feast of the First Fruits was that weekend and people flocked to the feast from the surrounding area. No less than seventeen nationalities of people were present in Jerusalem that day. God performed a mighty miracle. Every person present heard the disciples' message in their own native tongue. What a marvelous example of the reaching nature of God's love! It was no coincidence that the gift of the Spirit was poured out during the Feast of the First Fruits. The first fruit was multi-cultural and not only Jewish. It was an indication of what was to come!

Obviously, the Holy Spirit was the answer to Jesus plea to wait. Now that the gift of the Spirit was given it was time to reach the world with the Good News of life through relationship with Jesus. Three thousand entered relationship with Jesus that day. What could be clearer than the truth that they existed for the purpose of reaching others?

they stayed

They rejoiced that God was work. Their needs were being met. It was an exciting time. Good things were happening all around. The church was born and it was off to a great start. As a result, they stayed in Jerusalem.

The scriptures say, *God added to the church every day.*[8]

In the next chapter of the book of Acts, there was a mighty miracle of healing and more opportunities came to tell the story. So they stayed in Jerusalem. Culturally it was a fit for them. God was at work there. It was convenient. It was familiar. It was also a decision to ignore the command to go into all the world.

The next chapter brought more miracles and more opportunities to reach their own people. It was really exciting. They had clashes with the authorities, and they experienced God's supernatural provision. They were winning! What could be better?

The next chapter's story was, *more and more disciples believed* and they stayed in Jerusalem.

The next chapter recorded, *the believers rapidly multiplied* and they stayed in Jerusalem.[10]

The next chapter came, and they stayed in Jerusalem. Are you getting the picture? Wrap your arms around yourself and sing with me, rock slightly from side to side as you sing, *Jesus loves me, yes, Jesus loves me!* At this rate, how would the message get out to the world?

The next chapter begins with these words, *A great wave of persecution rose, the believers were scattered to Jerusalem, Judea, Samaria and eventually to the ends of the earth and they preached the Gospel wherever they went.*[11]

Finally they took the message to the world, but it was born more out of desperation than inspiration. They received the Holy Spirit in chapter two, but they didn't live as *SENT* people until they had no choice in chapter eight. God didn't cause the persecution, but he allowed it to accomplish his purposes.

what will it take?

This begs the question, what will it take, in your life and in my life, for us to live *SENT* lives? How many adventures will you have in missing the point? It isn't like this taking-the-Good-News-to-the-world thing is optional. You, like the Jews, are God's chosen. You are blessed to be a blessing. It is not about you. You joined a family with redemption as its' primary motivation.

Say it with me: *We are the people of God sent on a mission to share His light and love until the whole world knows.*

Ultimately, He will only work with churches and individuals who choose to live *SENT*. The scary part is that if an individual or a church wants to live their Christian life selfishly God will let them and their redemptive potential is squandered.

Remember, God gave the Israelites what they wanted when they refused to fight for the Promised Land, but in granting their request He also gave them leanness in their soul. He gave them what they wanted, and when they got it they were soul sick.

Maybe part of the problem is that we've learned the wrong song as the primary song of our youth. There is another song we should have learned first. The words are very similar, but the focus is entirely different.

This song goes like this:

Jesus loves the little children,
all the children of the world.
Red and yellow, black and white,
they are precious in his sight.
Jesus loves the little children of the world.

It is true that Jesus loves me, but it is also true that he loves the little children of the world. He wants me to give my life to live *SENT* so that everyone can know the love of Jesus.

Which song are you singing? Which one best describes the focus of your life.

Let's say the mission statement again, *We are the people of God sent on a mission to share His light and love until the whole world knows.* This is what it means to live *SENT.*

let's pray

God forgive me for my reflex decision to filter everything in my life according to how it affects me as if it was all about me. Remind me that I am chosen and blessed to be a blessing. Disturb me, if necessary, to keep me from seeking only after a comfortable and a convenient lifestyle. I pray the prayer of Isaiah, "Here am I, send me!"[12]

wrong song, chapter 15
questions for thought or discussion

1. Can you remember the first time you heard the song, *Jesus Loves Me*? Was it the first Christian song you heard?

2. Review the miracles of Exodus. Which ones best revealed the power of God?

3. Can you imagine how easy it would be to think that the point of the miracles was to deliver God's chosen people from slavery as an end instead of a means to an end?

4. Does it surprise you that Jesus would act so passionately when he cleansed the temple?

5. How would it have made the Gentiles feel to attempt to worship in a crowded marketplace?

6. What message did God intend to communicate to the world by pouring out his Holy Spirit on the day of Pentecost?

7. Did the early church realize they were blessed to be a blessing? Do you?

footnotes

1. Exodus 32
2. Hebrews 12:2
3. Mark 11:15-17
4. Mark 11:17A
5. Mark 11:17B
6. Acts 1:8B
7. Acts 1:8A
8. Acts 2:47 NIV
9. Acts 5:14
10. Acts 6:1
11. Acts 8:1
12. Isaiah 6:8

appendix

This circle illustrates the process of one finding their way back to God and becoming like Jesus. You could enter the circle at any of the three sections because they are three parts of the same whole. When someone accepts the forgiveness and grace of Jesus they are a new creation in Jesus. They are re-made to look like Him. There will be a part of their heart that beats fast with new love for God. They may be surprised to find a renewed love for other people. It may be an outright shock to feel a desire to live out the love of Jesus in mission. The result of these new desires cooperating together will produce a new purpose in life. Instead of living for self the Christ follower will become most like Jesus when all these are working together to create the on-purpose living we call living SENT.

As soon as one makes that all important choice the goal is to "follow" or grow to be like Jesus. We do that through learning to Love God, Love People and Live Out the love of Jesus. The arrows imply this is an on-going process. It is not linear. At times one may be stronger at the devotional side of life we call Loving God. Other times there may be an increased desire to live in community and Love People. And at a different time one may find themselves growing more through Living Out the love of Jesus through service. Together, these three catalysts for spiritual growth produce the life that is most like Jesus, a life that is SENT.

To find out more about Gary Kendall and the
Spiritual Growth Initiative, *30 Days to Living Sent*,
Please visit www.GaryKendall.org
and click on the SENT logo.

about the author

Gary Kendall has a deep passion for helping people find their way back to God and for planting and developing churches that do the same. Gary and his wife, Belinda, founded Indian Creek Community Church in 1985, which has grown from a home Bible study to a multi-site church. Gary serves Indian Creek as the Lead Pastor.

It's that passion that led him to co-found the Church Multiplication Association in 2004 (now Healthy Growing Churches Multiplication). Gary is also the President of Project Partner, a 501c3 charity, which supports mission ministry to China to touch hearts and transform communities there.

He invests time in the community through service on several local and national boards and frequently travels as a speaker/ conference leader nationally and internationally. Gary has co-authored two books, *Path to Power* with Pastor Jim Davey and *The Call to Love* with Belinda Kendall.

Gary and Belinda live in Olathe, Kansas and have three married children: Kristen (Josh), Jeremy (Jesi), and Luke (Rachel) and two grandchildren, Landon and Morgan.

计划 伙伴
project partner

Right now the gospel is spreading faster in China than anywhere else in the world! You can be part of this great revival. Join Project Partner to meet needs for water, education and medical care. Together we'll make an impact by demonstrating God's love in China.

Visit www.projectpartner.org/backwards today to learn what you can do.